OPERATION
FUNCTION ANALYSIS

Do It Yourself
Productivity Improvement

OPERATION FUNCTION ANALYSIS

Do It Yourself Productivity Improvement

Wm. Bruce Bumbarger

VAN NOSTRAND REINHOLD COMPANY
NEW YORK   CINCINNATI   TORONTO   LONDON   MELBOURNE

Library of Congress Catalog Card Number: 83-6918
ISBN: 0-442-21424-3

Manufactured in the United States of America

Published by Van Nostrand Reinhold Company Inc.
135 West 50th Street
New York, New York 10020

Van Nostrand Reinhold Company Limited
Molly Millars Lane
Wokingham, Berkshire RG11 2PY, England

Van Nostrand Reinhold
480 Latrobe Street
Melbourne, Victoria 3000, Australia

Macmillan of Canada
Division of Gage Publishing Limited
164 Commandar Boulevard
Agincourt, Ontario MIS 3C7, Canada

Library of Congress Cataloging in Publication Data

Bumbarger, William Bruce.
  Operation function analysis.

  Includes index.
  1. Productivity, Industrial. 2. Industrial productivity.
I. Title.
T58.8.B85   1983   653.5'1   83-6918
ISBN 0-442-21424-3

Preface

During the past decade, we have seen an enthusiastic shift from the old, authoritarian methods to the new participative approaches to productivity improvement. This is especially significant in the office, knowledge work areas, where people have a desire and a right to be involved in improving the performance of their own activities.

However, in addition to enthusiasm and desire, new skills are also needed. Over the past several years, we have developed O.F.A., a new do-it-yourself approach to productivity improvement, applicable in many areas, and especially useful in the office, knowledge sector. It combines elements of industrial engineering with the behavioral sciences. A number of users have encouraged me to put this method before the public, sharing in my belief that there is a need for a how-to manual on practical methods of productivity improvement. This book is my attempt to fill that need.

William Bruce Bumbarger
Atlanta, Georgia

Acknowledgments

I wish to thank the many managers, supervisors and workers with whom I have had contact, first in General Electric, and now as an independent consultant, and especially those who have used and contributed to the development of the O.F.A. method. Their practical contributions have become a part of this book.

Most of all, I want to recognize and thank Susan M. Bumbarger, my wife and colleague, who has worked closely with me in writing this book. Her many suggestions and editing were invaluable.

Contents

OPERATION
FUNCTION ANALYSIS

Do It Yourself
Productivity Improvement

Part I
The Logic of Operation
Function Analysis

Introduction

Operation Function Analysis (O.F.A.) is a participative, do-it-yourself productivity improvement method, applicable throughout the whole organization, and especially useful in the knowledge work areas and the activities they interface with.

O.F.A. combines in a new way many features of tested improvement methods with unique elements of its own. It draws on the concept of function first stressed by Larry Miles of General Electric, "father" of Value Analysis. It includes analysis techniques similar to those used by industrial engineers, as well as motivational factors that are the stock-in-trade of industrial psychologists. It embraces group creativity techniques that have recently been formalized in the Nominal Group Technique. Some have called O.F.A. the next step beyond Quality Circles, since circles typically focus on the more straightforward challenges within a relatively small group, whereas O.F.A. addresses challenges that are more complex and may span the total organization.

This book describes Operation Function Analysis. It is a how-to book — very short on elegant theories, no equations, no measurement theory, few footnotes and references, no bibliography. All the missing paraphernalia are available from other excellent sources.

Rather, this is a practical book, based on the experience of companies that have used O.F.A. since it was developed and refined in the late 1970s. Although the book is primarily concerned with Operation Function Analysis, the basic ideas here can be lifted out and made a part of your productivity improvement efforts regardless of the specific techniques you use.

Part 1 (Chapters 1–7) focuses on the logic of O.F.A., that is, why we need it, and why it works as it does. It gives just enough theory to enable you to take a new, more creative look at the activities of your organization, understand what you see, and determine what you should do about it.

Part 2 (Chapters 8–13) is concerned with the O.F.A. method. It gives a detailed, step-by-step description of how you can use O.F.A. to improve the productivity of your organization, from the first planning by senior management through the implementation of your improvement recommendations.

Part 3 (Chapters 14–18) presents five case studies which illustrate the logic and method. These examples will allow you to learn from the experience of others who have used Operation Function Analysis.

Chapter 1

Ho Hum! Why Bother With This?

It seems as if every day yet another author or speaker is urging us to become more productive, dazzling us with shocking statistics and authoritative statements. Recently, we have been counseled to shift our attention from the factory to the office, from blue collar to white collar workers.

These overly simple labels — factory, office, white collar, blue collar — tend to conceal the real character of a major transition that is occurring in our country. They can even handicap our productivity improvement efforts.

What is this real transition? It is twofold. First, there is a broad shift from routine, manual work to knowledge work, in *all areas* of business and government, at *every level* of the organization. Second, there is a related shift from the old, *authoritarian* methods of management to the more *participative* approaches.

SHIFT TO KNOWLEDGE WORK

All of us devote some of our time to knowledge work. The laborer digging that ditch for sewer repairs devotes nearly all his time to routine, manual work. Yet he still must examine and evaluate the firmness of the sidewalls of the ditch, judge the best place to throw the dirt, measure the depth of the ditch, and perform other knowledge activities.

In a typical equipment manufacturing business, major knowledge work activities can consume nearly half the costs of operation, and *more* than half the total order processing cycle time. In other businesses and government agencies, this share can rise to essentially 100%. In short, more and more of us are becoming knowledge workers, regardless of where we work, or the color of our collars. For this reason, we need to concentrate more of our productivity improvement efforts on these knowledge activities, wherever they occur, whomever they involve.

SHIFT TO PARTICIPATION

Traditional time study and work measurement methods, and similar authoritarian approaches developed in the past for routine, manual work, are not adequate for knowledge work. New methods are needed for several reasons:

Knowledge Workers Are Involved Workers

Because of their training and exposure, knowledge workers want to and are able to participate in the decisions that affect their activities. Productivity improvement methods used here should recognize and capitalize on their interest and skill.

Knowledge Work Is Not Repetitive

Individual decisions are made by the worker as the work progresses. Any given operation may not be repeated for days, weeks, or ever. Because of this, we must focus our productivity improvement efforts at a higher level than we do on the more routine, manual activities. We must view the work flow in terms of major work functions, rather than smaller, detailed operations, and we must concentrate on the demands that cause us to perform these functions.

Knowledge Activities Are Organizationally Complex

During the course of his work, a person who performs routine, manual tasks normally contacts only a few immediate associates — his supervisor, an inspector, the person next to him on the assembly line, someone at the other end of the office.

In contrast, knowledge work is much more organizationally complex. A typical knowledge worker may contact people in many other departments in the organization, as well as external groups. For example, a design engineer may contact people in field sales, manufacturing, accounting, service parts. The supermarket manager may contact his company's warehouse, specialty salesman, a union representative, a city councilman. Productivity improvement methods for knowledge activities must recognize these complexities and deal with them.

Changes Here Cause Improvements Over There

The traditional improvement methods used on routine, manual work focus on and seek savings in the immediate activities. That is, the changes and the resulting improvements both occur in the same area.

For instance, if you want to improve the performance of a group of clerks who perform repetitive tasks, you focus directly on these tasks, increase their efficiency, and expect to see a reduction of clerical effort in that same area of the organization.

However, because of the interorganizational complexities mentioned before, changes in knowledge work activities in one area often result in greater improvements in other distant areas, such as direct labor, material, purchased services, etc. We call this knowledge worker leverage.

Example. An equipment manufacturing business spent 13 million dollars a year on direct materials used in the production of its products. Nine buyers in the purchasing organization placed purchase orders for these materials with vendors.

As a result of their Operation Function Analysis program, changes were identified in the purchasing process which could result in the reduction of buying effort by over 160 man-hours a month, or approximately one person's effort.

One possibility might have been to immediately remove the "surplus" buyer from these activities, the resulting reduction of personnel bringing about an annual savings of approximately $25,000 a year. Sound fine?

But wait! Further analysis by the O.F.A. team showed that this same "surplus" buyer could be retained within the purchasing organization, and assigned to develop improved methods for identifying and negotiating with better vendors. They further estimated that these new methods, when used by all buyers, would result in at least 2% reduction in material costs, or about $260,000 a year.

Question: Is it better to harvest the $25,000 annual savings in the purchasing organization, or the $260,000 annual savings in the direct material purchases? Guess which option this business picked!

Example. This same business had a customer service organization. Four people in it devoted their full time to analyzing customer claims for damaged, defective, and missing materials associated with products shipped to customers. These claims totaled about $940,000 a year.

The O.F.A. team reviewed these activities, and identified changes in the process that would reduce the required effort in that department by eighty man-hours per month, about one-half of one person's time, valued at about $13,000 per year.

As the O.F.A. team pursued this further, they identified ways that one of these analysts could devote half his effort to improving the analysis process, and as a result the company could reduce the total claims expense by at least 10%, or $94,000 per year.

Question: Should the company harvest the $13,000 annual savings within the customer service department, or the $94,000 savings in external expenses? Which would you pick?

Productivity improvement methods should recognize this leverage effect. That is, changes in knowledge work activities often can result in much greater savings in other, even distant areas of the business.

SUMMARY

Ho Hum! Why bother with this? Here's why. The knowledge work content of essentially all jobs is increasing, in all areas of our organizations. We must focus our productivity improvement efforts on this knowledge work wherever it occurs.

Authoritarian methods developed for routine, manual work are not adequate for knowledge activities. New, more participative methods must be used which recognize the special characteristics of knowledge work, and encourage people to be responsible for their own productivity improvement efforts.

Chapter 2
Do It Yourself — The Best Way

For years, productivity improvement was largely authoritarian. The senior executives told the subordinate line managers what changes to make, word was passed down the ladder until lower level people implemented the changes. That was that.

If that did not work, then technical experts from the "outside" were called in — external consultants, corporate staff members, etc. They would study the activities of the business, evaluate what they saw, and then present their recommendations to the senior operating managers. Although subordinate line managers might have serious reservations, they were directed to implement the outside expert's recommendations without question.

More recently we have seen a major increase in the use of participative improvement methods in which employees at all levels work together to make their own activities more productive. Examples include Quality Circles, Nominal Group Technique, and Operation Function Analysis.

This confirms the first rule for productivity improvement in the professional, knowledge office area:

Rule 1: Lasting productivity improvement must come from within, and cannot be effectively imposed from the outside.

ADVANTAGES TO THE ORGANIZATION

The do-it-yourself approach to productivity improvement has many advantages, both to the organization that uses it, and to the people involved in such programs. Here are some of the advantages to the organization.

Uses the Best Knowledge

Your own people know more about their day-by-day work than anyone else. We've all heard it said, and it is true: you could walk out into any department of your business, give the first person you meet a blank sheet of paper, and ask him to list a half dozen ways to make his job more productive. In ten minutes you will have six good ideas. Your own people see what needs to be done to improve productivity. All they need is encouragement, and ways to organize their ideas and convert them into action.

Gets the Best Results

Since your own people have the best knowledge, and results are based on knowledge, the do-it-yourself approach will produce the best results.

Eliminates the N.I.H. Factor

Since the improvement recommendations will be made by your own people, they will view the improvement program as theirs, not some outsider's. The "not invented here" factor will be greatly reduced, and necessary changes will be made more easily. Experience in Japan confirms this. There, the people who will be affected by the outcome thoroughly identify and analyze the problem, and derive and plan the changes. As a result, they can more rapidly and effectively implement a successful solution.

Increases Lasting Commitment to Productivity

Through their participation in a do-it-yourself program, your own people will become committed to productivity improvement. They will be there in the future to ensure that their changes are permanent. As a result, the benefits will be more lasting.

ADVANTAGES TO THE PEOPLE

Perhaps the greatest advantage of the participative, do-it-yourself approach is that it benefits the people as well as the process. Over the past several years, we have surveyed participants in do-it-yourself improvement programs, and have asked them to list the benefits they personally received from their participation. Here is what they said.

Improves Communications

Too often we think of communications as the employee bulletin board, or the division newsletter. Communication is much more than this. It is people working together to achieve solutions to common problems, and they get this through participative productivity improvement programs.

Spreads Knowledge

The more you know about your job, the better you can do it. If your job involves interorganizational activities, as most knowledge work does, you should know as much as you can about all departments with which you interface. People get this knowledge as they work together to improve the performance of their business.

Increases Integrative Attitude

Many organizations are handicapped by parochial attitudes and practices. In many ways, each department within the business competes with the others. Managers protect their empires. When people from different areas of the business work together to improve the productivity of the whole business, they always experience lasting improvement in their integrative attitude, and find that it is easier to work together in the future.

Improves Motivation and Morale

Many people work for years with minimum motivation, just "holding down" a job. However, when you ask that same person to help *improve* the business, it tells him that you respect his opinion, and that you believe he can do more than just his day-by-day work. It enriches his job, increases his motivation, and boosts his morale.

PARTICIPATION – HOW TO GET IT

Clearly, these participative, do-it-yourself, approaches have many advantages, and more and more companies want to use them in their productivity improvement programs.

However – and here's the catch – an organization cannot have temporary participation. You cannot conduct a successful improvement program based on employee participation *if* the overall company philosophy is based on authoritarian attitudes and practices. Participative improvement programs work *only* when employee participation is a continuing way of life within the business, not just a transient attitude turned on whenever management wants people to "work on" productivity improvement.

Therefore, our real challenge is not just to get a few employees involved in a single productivity improvement program. Rather, it is to establish employee participation throughout all activities of the organization. Only then can we hope to achieve real, lasting productivity improvement.

How can the managers within an organization foster and encourage such broad participation? Let's describe several factors which contribute to effective employee participation, and illustrate them with the case of a company whose management attitudes and practices include many of these factors.

There are many such success stories for employee participation, and we continually hear about the industry giants with essentially limitless resources, and grand programs. But the typical business manager often finds it hard to relate to these businesses. So this time let's look at an ordinary, medium-size company, the RTE Corporation of Waukesha, Wisconsin.

RTE Corporation is a producer of electrical products for power distribution systems and industry, with distribution and power transformers accounting for over half its approximately $200 million annual sales.

Founded in 1947, RTE has grown rapidly, and now has about 3,000 people in 11 domestic and foreign facilities, plus sales offices and warehouses. It values its employees, and emphasizes employee commitment and participation in all aspects of the business.

Sounds like an ordinary company, doesn't it? It is, except that throughout this rapid growth, RTE has maintained and improved its productivity – largely based on strong employee participation – until it is now nearly 30% more productive than the average durable goods manufacturer in its size range, based on annual output per employee! RTE accomplished this in the face of a very strong competition from much larger, firmly entrenched, long established businesses, often in periods of market softness. Clearly, employee participation works!

Now let's look at some of the factors that make it work.

Management Commitment

The management of the organization is totally committed to the complete utilization of human resources, and to full employee participation. It is a real commitment, at all levels from the president to the first line supervisor, supported by formally stated and closely administered policies.

This commitment to employee participation is a conscious part of every manager's and supervisor's job. He must demonstrate this commitment by actions such as the steps described here, and he will be evaluated on the basis of his performance. Management knows that lip service alone is worse than nothing, will be seen through immediately, and will harm the overall performance of the business.

Management Availability

One of the best ways to demonstrate a commitment to employee participation and involvement is for management at all levels to be visible and available to all employees. There are no ivory towers. The open door is not just a policy, it is mandatory practice.

Furthermore, managers don't just sit in their offices like spiders in their webs, almost challenging employees to walk through that door. Rather, they demonstrate their availability by going out into the office and factories and *initiating* the contacts. Workers at all levels know their managers.

To illustrate, a visitor drove up to see RTE's executive vice president. The visitor noticed several factory workers sitting outside, eating their lunch. He asked: "Where are the executive offices?" One of the workmen asked, "Who do you want to see?" Visitor: "Mr. Lane." Worker: "Oh, sure. His office is over in that building.

Go around to the other side and in the door, up two floors, turn to the left, and ask for him. I think he's up there now. I haven't seen him go out yet."

This workman knew who the "big boss" was, where his office was located, and even that he probably was there at that moment. That's visibility! It was immediately clear that the company was a team, and this man felt he was a part of it.

Communications: Direct, Open, Honest

To be successful, communications must be complete — the whole picture. Except for obvious legal and commercial considerations, RTE employees hear all about the company's operations: the successes and failures, the good decisions and the bad ones, the good news and the bad.

The visibility and availability of managers and supervisors establishes an environment for good communications and encourages continual, informal contacts and discussions, through which much information is passed.

The principal formal channel of communications, however, is a series of regular employee meetings. During the first month in each quarter, senior managers hold meetings with all employees. Twenty such meetings occur in the Waukesha area, with similar meetings at other locations.

Each meeting involves a different group of people, such as a department or function, with common interests and problems. All employees, except first line supervisors, in the group attend, along with senior division and corporate executives. Information is presented on company activities, and employees are encouraged to present comments and ask questions, either directly or through representatives they select. Questions are answered by the appropriate executive, on the spot if possible, followed up later if necessary. Minutes are published, including answers to all questions. These answers then become a management commitment for action.

During the second month of each quarter, divisional meetings are held, similar in format and general content to the general management meetings, but focusing on divisional concerns, and conducted by the division general manager and his staff.

In the third month of each quarter, departmental "tool box" meetings are held by first line supervisors with all factory employees in the Waukesha area. These typically are concerned with more specific, detailed problems within their own department.

Through these three levels of meetings, employees in the RTE Waukesha plants are able to communicate freely and directly with all levels of management at least once every quarter. Similar opportunities are provided at other domestic and Canadian locations. In these formal meetings, and in the many informal contacts between employees and managers, communications are direct, open, and honest, and form a solid basis for real employee participation and involvement in the business.

Let People Be Involved in Decisions That Affect Them

The day of the shuffling worker, hat in hand, is ending — for which we should be forever thankful. Modern employees want to participate in the decisions that affect them, and they have every right to, for two reasons: their commitment, and their knowledge.

One still hears hard-shell managers say: "Why should I listen to them? They're employees, they just work here — here today, gone tomorrow. They don't have any real commitment to this business."

Wrong. Look at the typical business. With the exception of closely held companies, the average shareholder has no lasting commitment to the company. He can cut his connections with a call to his broker.

Senior managers are very mobile, easily moving from one division or company to another, following the call of the corporate directors or the executive recruiter.

The employee, however, often is here to stay: the order desk clerk, the draftsperson, the inventory control specialist, the cost analyst, the shipping foreman. They have made a full commitment, usually for an extended period, to this business. Based on this commitment, they have as much right as anyone else to be involved in the decisions that affect them, probably more.

Modern employees have a right to be heard for another reason: their knowledge. The average worker knows more about his own job than anyone else.

Example. Too often in industry, a highly educated industrial engineer establishes a method and sets a production standard for a factory operation. When he goes back to his office, the machine operator takes over and quickly figures out a better, more efficient way that beats the standard all to pieces, often to a point where he has to control and conceal his own output to avoid an "audit." (*Note:* This is *not* a problem at RTE, which has a well planned and controlled incentive system.)

Example. Quality circles are in place all over the country, and in them employees are identifying better ways to do their jobs.

Example. Using O.F.A., people who do the work have derived more productive ways of working which have been missed for years by outside experts.

In summary, let people be involved in the decisions that affect them because (1) they have a desire and commitment to be involved, and (2) they can bring knowledge to the decisions not available anywhere else.

Demonstrate Mutual Respect by Listening to Each Other

Managers need to listen to employees for the two reasons described above: Employees have a right to be heard, and they have good knowledge to be shared.

However, listening takes skill as well as will. For years we have had courses in public speaking, and all rising young people were expected to participate in them. At last we have established courses in *listening*. Does your organization have a program to develop listening skills?

Caution. Too often, listening skill programs focus on the need for managers to listen to employees. Equally important is the need for employees to listen to managers, and members of all groups to listen to each other.

Get Those Involved in a Process to Talk with Each Other

This idea is not new; it has been around for years. It works well if the process (1) is clearly defined, and (2) occurs all within a relatively small organization.

However, most important processes are not well defined, and they often span more than one group. In these cases, we must take special steps to talk to each other directly and to pierce the barriers that too often separate organizations.

For example, RTE shop employees regularly participate in solving specific problems. Recently a problem arose involving transformer parts used in the Waukesha assembly operation, but which were initially fabricated at another company plant out of state. Rather than sending the typical negotiating team of managers and technicians, management sent several production line employees from the Waukesha assembly plant to discuss the situation with the manager and people at the out-of-state plant. RTE tries to eliminate all filters between the people who have first-hand knowledge of a problem in a process, and the persons who have the responsibility and authority to correct it.

Invest in Training

One of the best ways to get employees really involved in the business is to train them well at all levels. Here are three cases which illustrate how RTE does this.

1. They have developed a closed-circuit television system with a tape library covering most factory jobs with significant learning curves. This has reduced the training time on a complex coil winding operation from approximately 20 weeks to 5 weeks. The reject rate during training has gone from a very high level to virtually zero.

Tapes produced in the main plant in Waukesha can also be used to introduce new products and processes at branch plants. For instance, when the company started up a components plant in Taiwan, specially produced tapes were used to train newly hired operators in the plant. Later, the audio portions of the tapes were translated into French and used in training at their new plant in France.

2. Another case involves supervisor training. Too often we see situations in which a good machinist or assembly worker is made a foreman. Lacking leadership skills, and even knowledge of the day-by-day duties of a foreman, he fails. Only then do we send him through foreman training.

RTE has an active *pre*-supervisory training program which is available to all shop and nonexempt office employees who are interested in supervision as a career. This creates a pool of potential candidates available and motivated when a shift leader, foreman, or office supervisor job opens up.

3. RTE has a broad tuition refund program open to *all* employees. This covers specific courses related to one's job, as well as general development programs leading to a certificate, Bachelor's Degree, or an advance degree such as an MBA.

When employees see that the company has made this kind of commitment in training them, they in turn will make a commitment to the company, and increase their involvement in the business.

Eliminate Class Distinctions and Adversarial Relationships

Nothing dampens employee participation more than artificial class distinctions, and the resulting "us versus them," adversarial attitudes too frequently found in business and government organizations.

We've all seen examples of wasteful competitiveness between departments in a business. I have even heard business managers talk about the need for "checks and balances" in their organizations, for example, the need for engineering to "keep those guys up in sales straightened out," for sales to "follow up" on manufacturing, for manufacturing to keep an eye on engineering, and for accounting to check up on everyone.

RTE has no status symbols, and strives for equality among all classes of workers in all departments. No corporate country clubs, no plush management offices, no company cars (except where needed for field activities), no lavish executive perquisites. There are no reserved parking places except for the plant nurse and the mail truck at any location.

Everything possible is done to eliminate artificial walls between departments. Recreation and social activities, picnics and parties, are handled by employees involved, and are open to all employees. There are no separate office and factory functions, no "office versus shop" baseball games, no separate bowling leagues, etc.

As a result, all employees can feel they are a part of the "first" team, and share equally in a commitment to the business.

SUMMARY

Is it easy to achieve real employee participation in your organization, without significant problems? Mr. A. J. Lane, Senior Vice President of RTE, has this to say:

The answer is clearly no, since nothing really worthwhile is very easy to achieve. A management-employee relationship of the type practiced by RTE requires the absolute commitment of all managers and executives to the total corporate philosophy. Internally, we live in a fishbowl where all of our decisions and actions are clearly visible to all employees. RTE managers are human beings, and as such, make human errors, but there is no place to hide when this happens. We admit our mistakes, discuss our problems, and we are better managers because of it.

Does improvement through employee participation really work? Just remember the 30% productivity advantage.

Chapter 3
Obstacles to Innovation

In the preceding chapter, we discussed the advantages of the do-it-yourself, participative approach, in which people throughout the organization become involved in productivity improvement activities.

When a senior executive first considers using these participative methods, he often says something like this:

> Yes, I like the idea of all our people participating in performance improvement. It sounds great. But these are the same people who have worked here for years, doing the same old thing, the same old way. They have a lot of biases, a lot of old habits. What hope is there that they will come up with something new and more productive?

The answer lies in the second rule of productivity improvement:

Rule 2: Real, lasting productivity improvement requires change. And change requires creativity, innovation.

A really creative attitude will allow people in an organization to do two things in their productivity improvement programs. First, it will enable them to come up with really new solutions to old problems. Second, it will enable them to evaluate these solutions without the constraint of old habits and biases.

Therefore, it is essential that through our O.F.A. training, we do three things:

- Recognize and remove mental obstacles to creativity which could keep us from achieving our productivity improvement goals (this chapter).

- Develop positive, creative attitudes on which to base our productivity improvement efforts (Chapter 4).
- Learn creative skills for use in this work (Chapter 4).

Mental obstacles fall into four broad categories: perceptual, habit, cultural, and emotional obstacles. If they are recognized, we can work with and overcome them and move on to really effective productivity improvement.

PERCEPTUAL OBSTACLES

Everyone of us has heard about some new invention or solution to a nagging problem and said to himself: "Hm! That's clever, but it's not all *that* great. I could have figured out the solution myself. But, I didn't realize *that* was the problem."

In other words, perceptual obstacles are those practices and attitudes that prevent us from clearly seeing the problem in the first place. And if you don't see it, you surely cannot solve it. Here are some common perceptual obstacles.

Cannot Distinguish Between Causes and Effects

As described later (Chapter 5), productivity efforts in the past frequently focused on details of work flow, saving ten minutes here, fifteen there. Yet these same improvement efforts often ignored the effect of the demands that drove this work flow. That is, the program focused on the effects (work flow details), not on the causes (driving demands).

As you will read in Chapter 7, this becomes even more of a problem in interorganizational work flow, where the cause may occur in one department and the effect in another.

Many of our problems in productivity improvement result from our inability to distinguish between causes and effects.

Problem Scope Too Narrow

Too often we try to solve a problem without adequately recognizing its setting or surrounding environment. For example, management in one company thought they had a problem involving production scheduling of product parts and subassemblies. But on more thorough examination, they found the problem involved the way these product parts and subassemblies were recorded on the engineering bills of material. On even further examination, they found the problem also involved how the product was structured to include these components. What appeared to be a relatively narrow, focused problem turned out to be a much broader, more complex one.

Recognize Only the Obvious

Sometimes the more we know about a situation, the harder it is to solve it in a really creative manner. We continue to view the issue in the same old way. We look at the problem, without really seeing all aspects of it.

Years ago, Charles Kettering, the great inventor and automobile executive, worked in Detroit, Michigan, yet drove to his home in Dayton, Ohio, on weekends. He commented to his associates that he could make the trip in four and one-half hours. One of them who also lived in Dayton challenged him:

Friend: I don't believe it.

Kettering: But I do it every so often with no problem.

Friend: But I'm a much better driver than you are, and I can't do it.

Kettering: I'm going down this Friday afternoon. Why not ride along in my car with me and see?

So they rode together to Dayton in Kettering's car in about four and one-half hours. But the friend was mad as anything, and he said: "Hell, no wonder you can do it in four and one-half hours. You didn't stay on Route 25!"

Now back then, Route 25 was the red line on the map that marked the main road between Detroit and Dayton. Kettering's friend was very familiar with that main road, and it never occurred to him that you could take any other road on either side of Route 25.

As Kettering later wrote, "There was a lot of country on either side of Route 25; in fact, half of the earth was on each side of it!" His friend saw only the obvious, and failed to see all the other possibilities — half the world on either side.

So as you seek to make your organizations more productive, watch out for perceptual blocks to innovation. If you can't see the problem, you surely can't solve it.

HABIT OBSTACLES

We humans learned an early lesson about habit from our insect friends, the processionary caterpillars. These insects crawl through pine trees, eating the needles, all the while moving in a long procession. One caterpillar leads, and all others follow, each with his eyes half closed, and nose pressed against the hind end of the one in front.

Back in the late 1800s, Jean Henri Fabre, the great French naturalist, believed that insects were controlled by reasoned intelligence, rather than habit. To demonstrate this, Fabre conducted an experiment with processionary caterpillars.

He coaxed a group of these insects to form a procession around the rim of a large flower pot. The first one connected to the last one — a full circle moving around the rim — no beginning nor end.

Fabre felt that shortly the reasoned intelligence of these insects would catch on, take over, and the caterpillars would break the circle, and move over into the lush green pine needles on nearby trees.

They did not! Around and around they went, without let-up, for seven days and nights, until finally they dropped from exhaustion and starvation, broke their circle, and fell off the rim of the pot. Fabre was sure that insects were controlled by reasoned intelligence not habit, but his experiment demonstrated the exact opposite.

Well, you say, that's fine for bugs, but we are humans, not bugs. Maybe so. But let's look at our own organizations. They are full of processionary caterpillars, as shown in Figure 3.1.

Years ago, someone expressed an opinion, and away we went. We followed that opinion and formed a beaten path. This established experience, which grew into habit. It matured into custom, and then evolved into a tradition.

By this time we were pretty solid. We couldn't break a tradition, after all. Neither could we admit being controlled by traditions, so we renamed them and called them present methods. The following year, we documented them, called them standards, and put them in a big black notebook. Once they were standards, there was great resis-

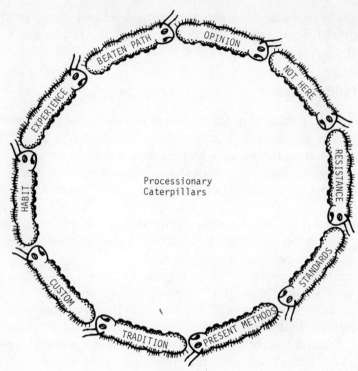

Processionary
Caterpillars

Figure 3.1

tance to change, culminating in the "no — absolutely not here" response. And it all began with just someone's opinion.

Fabre's processionary caterpillars fed on pine needles. What do our caterpillars feed on? They relish the negative attitudes and responses to change so often heard in many companies, and here is a list of some of them:

"It's been done this way for years — why change?"
"That's been tried before, and it didn't work then."
"Our business is different."
"We'll come back to it later."
"It leaves me cold."
"Let's think about it some more."
"This isn't the right time for it."
"We can't hold up production for that."
"Cost is not important — just get it out the back door."
"We can't help it. It's policy, you know."

"We don't have enough time right now."
"We don't do it that way."
"It costs too much."
"That's not my responsibility."
"No one else knows as much about it as we do."

The beauty of this list is that it is in random order. You can start anywhere, and give the responses in any order. In fact, I almost guarantee that any five of them, taken in whatever order you wish, will enable you to kill the very best productivity improvement idea you have ever encountered!

So, in summary, if we are to achieve lasting improvement, we must get rid of the habits that block and stifle our creativity. We must squash the processionary caterpillars infesting our organizations, and eliminate the negative attitudes on which they feed.

CULTURAL OBSTACLES

Cultural obstacles to creativity are probably the most difficult to overcome because they are bred into us, and are a permanent part of our adult makeup, both as individuals and a society.

Napoleon Bonaparte told us, "Imagination rules the world." Yet, Charles Kettering warned us, "The possibilities a new idea opens up are not visualized because not one man in a thousand has imagination."

As youngsters we are innovative. But it is soon knocked out of us. Remember?

"Don't try it — you might fail."
"Don't question Grandpa — he knows best."
"Stay in your yard — you don't know what's over in that field."
"Don't taste it — the dog just licked it."
"Don't talk to them — they don't live near here."

Most of our creativity was trampled before we entered school. The educational system killed most of the remainder, and our first boss destroyed the rest. By the time we were twenty-five, ready to start up the ladder, our innovative skills were stifled by many cultural obstacles. Let's look at some of them.

The Desire to Conform

In most people, the desire to conform is simply overwhelming. To illustrate this, try this experiment at your next office meeting.

Before the meeting, compose a statement that you know is totally wrong, and that everyone at your meeting will also know is wrong.

Next, pick one person as the "victim." Then individually contact all the other people and:

1. Tell them you are going to conduct an experiment at the forthcoming meeting.
2. Tell them the incorrect statement you have composed.
3. Explain that you are going to bring up this incorrect statement at the meeting.
4. Instruct them to insist the statement is *correct,* even though they know that it is *incorrect.*

After everyone is seated at the meeting, somehow bring forth the incorrect statement, and ask for opinions around the table. One by one, the people in on the game will agree with the statement and insist it is correct. When you finally ask the victim for his comments, nine times out of ten he will seize up. Perhaps he will refuse to comment on the statement, or he may even join the crowd and say the statement is correct, even though down deep inside he is absolutely certain it is *incorrect.* Most of us simply have to conform, and this is a terrible obstacle to innovation.

Inquisitiveness Is Antisocial

Our society discourages inquisitiveness. We are suspicious of people asking questions. When this happens to us in business, we tell the person, "Mind your own business," or "That's not in your job description — don't worry about it."

Yet, as Henry Kissenger said, "Ask an impertinent question, get a pertinent answer!" So if you want to improve productivity through innovation, don't be afraid to ask questions.

Intuitive Thinking Is Weak Thinking

This is a major cultural obstacle. For centuries, Western civilization has favored solution of problems through detailed analysis. In our male dominated society, we have felt that reason, analysis, logic were strong characteristics, sought and expected in a man, and greatly preferred as a basis for decisions in business and government.

Moreover, we have viewed intuition as weak thinking, and often have referred to "woman's intuition." Traditionally, we have felt that such second rate, "female" thinking should never be used for serious decisions.

But wait. In Japan, as we have all read, intuitive thinking is greatly favored. Dr. E. Paul Torrance, of the University of Georgia, Athens, Georgia, in his studies of creativity in Japan, found over twice as many Japanese students as United States students viewed themselves as intuitive in thought process. Also, they preferred conditions that favor intuitive thinking rather than rational, logical thinking.

Dr. Torrance points out that Japan is a world leader in creativity, and that to a significant degree this creativity is a result of emphasis on intuitive thinking.

Our work with companies using Operation Function Analysis has demonstrated a need for both analytical and intuitive thinking in the productivity improvement process, and your improvement program should use them both. Chapters 11 and 12 discuss this further.

Groups Can't Innovate

For years, American business heroes have been the lonely, rugged individuals — Edison, Ford, Kaiser, Hughes, Firestone — and they served our country well.

As a result, many business managers believe groups cannot innovate, and even ridicule group efforts. Concensus management has been rejected as a sign of weakness. Many companies have a rule: "No Committees." We even see little plaques and signs in offices:

"A Camel Is a Horse Designed by a Committee."
"No One Ever Saw a Monument to a Committee."

Even the great innovator Kettering said, "Man is so constituted as to see what is wrong with a new thing, not what is right. To verify this, you have but to submit a new idea to a committee. They will obliterate 90% of rightness for the sake of 10% wrongness."

Yet some of the world's most effective industries — Japanese — use group innovation very successfully. Dr. Torrance describes how this begins with Japanese students who from earliest days participate in close-knit group activities — classroom, field trips, projects — during which they learn group innovation and problem solving methods. They learn to be sensitive to their peers, and to restrain personal egoism.

Dr. Torrance points out that they develop strong pride in the group, the family, school, community, company, and nation. Since the individual supports the group, and identifies with the group, it is perfectly acceptable for an individual to overachieve, because it is in support of his peers, and not his personal ego.

If American businesses are to regain world leadership in productivity growth, we must learn to more effectively work, think, plan and innovate in groups.

Fantasy Is a Waste of Time

In our society, fantasy often is viewed as a childish characteristic, or at best a trait of impractical dreamers. As a result of this cultural obstacle, productivity improvement ideas and recommendations often are small, even trivial: save a few forms here, save a few pencils there. We shy away from mind-boggling ideas.

We must remove this obstacle. We must engage in fantasy and dreaming, and develop audacious recommendations for improvement. It is easy to tone down a huge, outlandish idea; it is practically impossible to expand a small, trivial idea.

Premature Judgment

Most Western societies are composed of practical people, quick to seek immediate results, and to apply final judgments. Indeed, rapid decisions often are considered a mark of a good manager.

However, as we will see later in this chapter, and in Chapters 11 and 12, we can achieve better results in our productivity improvement work if we let ideas and recommendations flow out until we exhaust our creative store. Only then should we apply our judgment and decide which ideas should be implemented.

EMOTIONAL OBSTACLES

Let's see where we are. We have described three types of obstacles that prevent us from being really innovative in our productivity improvement work: perceptual, habit, and cultural. Let's move on to the fourth type, emotional. Here are a few of them.

N.I.H. Bias

All of us are biased to some degree against things that are not invented here. "After all," we say, "how could anyone else know more about our department than we do. We've been here twelve years. We've tried most everything we can to become more productive. Start your productivity program somewhere else, not here!"

There are two ways to handle this N.I.H. bias: Override it, or eliminate it. Those with a more authoritarian management style prefer simply to override it. Many external consultants, operation auditors, and analysts will stress their "independent, unbiased viewpoint," which they feel enables them to see problems and solutions that the internal people cannot see. These specialists will conduct their review of the assigned area, present their results to the senior managers, who in turn will tell their subordinates to implement the changes — or else.

This approach was heavily favored in the past. However, it has major limitations in the field of productivity improvement, especially in the knowledge areas. When productivity recommendations are made by outsiders, the internal people feel no pride of ownership, and often resist the implementation through foot dragging and disruptions. When you simply override bias, the bias is still there, stewing away beneath the surface.

Many senior managers now realize it is better to permanently *eliminate* the bias in their own people by teaching them to be more creative. This way they can view their activities with more open minds, and more easily accept the resulting changes. These new creative attitudes and skills are discussed in the next chapter.

Fear of Authority Figures

In ancient days, they killed the messenger who brought the bad news. Although we are not quite that harsh today, some businesses and government organizations still operate in an authoritarian fashion. This, coupled with our early upbringing, can instill in some people an unnatural fear of authority figures.

Even though we may know much more about a specific subject than he does, we cannot force ourselves to face up to the boss, explain why he is wrong, and what is right.

Sometimes this fear extends to *all* people. We simply cannot cross a person with a differing opinion. This yes-man attitude is a great obstacle to effective innovation and productivity improvement.

Fear of Making a Mistake

Kettering again has a lesson for us. He said, "Business decisions in the main are not based upon economic motives but rather upon the fear of personal loss. Fear of loss, not profit, dominates our business complex."

This still is true in many cases. Our fear of making a mistake, or of appearing foolish in the eyes of our peers, is a tremendous emotional obstacle against innovation. Real productivity improvement can be achieved only if we are willing to take the risk.

Compulsion for Immediate Success

Often a person is so hungry for visible success he will either jump on the first idea that comes along, or else give up if a solution does not appear immediately.

In most businesses today, the easy problems have already been solved. The remaining productivity improvement challenges are complex, and often require substantial study before they can be solved. Don't trip over the "immediate success" emotional obstacle. Go for the long haul.

Personal Security

All of us complain about the standard procedures, rules, and regulations which dictate how we should carry out our day-by-day work.

However, many people actually like these constraints because in clinging to clearly defined and well established standards they feel secure. New ideas, methods, and approaches threaten their personal security.

You cannot achieve real productivity improvement in this environment. Our experience with O.F.A. programs shows that people who worship security will seek improvements through small, predictable, well controlled changes. This is not satisfactory. Real improvement requires major, even audacious changes.

Private Turf

Every major organization is divided into departments, sections, and smaller groups. Each group's responsibilities are defined, and the people in it view these responsibilities as "theirs." They are naturally defensive of their home turf and the separating boundaries.

Since real improvement often focuses on interorganizational work flow, many of these organizational walls must be dented, even removed. If this is resisted, on the basis of defense of "private turf," then good creative improvement ideas will be lost.

SUMMARY

Improvement requires change, and change requires creativity, innovation. Yet there are many obstacles to innovation, in four broad categories: perceptual, habit, cultural, and emotional. We must recognize these obstacles and deal with them if we are to improve the productivity of our organizations. The next chapter describes how we can remove these obstacles through more creative attitudes and skills.

Chapter 4
Developing Creative
Attitudes and Skills

The preceding chapter describes obstacles which prevent us from being really creative in our productivity improvement activities. It is not enough just to recognize these blocks. We must adopt positive, creative attitudes to overcome them. Let's look to a different source for guidance.

CREATIVE ATTITUDES

Dr. Robert H. Schuller, Pastor of the Crystal Cathedral in Garden Grove, California, is one of the great Christian leaders of our country. He preaches on the need and value of positive attitudes in our lives, and has developed a set of Ten Commandments for Possibility Thinking.* Although Dr. Schuller does not present himself as a productivity expert, his commandments are excellent guides for us as we seek to become more creative in our productivity improvement programs.

Commandment #1

Never reject a possibility because you see something wrong with it!

There is something wrong with every good idea. . . . You don't throw away a suggestion when you see a problem. Instead, you isolate the problem from the possibility. You neutralize the negative. You exploit the possibility. . . .

---

*Dr. Robert Schuller, "The Ten Commandments for Possibility Thinking," *Let's Eliminate Negative Thinking,* Part 2, 1981, pp. 4–10.

Commandment #2

Never reject a possibility because you won't get the credit! . . . Don't worry about getting the credit. If you do, you'll become ego-involved in the decision-making moments of life. Decisions must never be based on ego needs. They must be based on others' needs and pressures that transcend your own desires. . . .

Commandment #3

Never reject an idea because it's impossible!

Almost every great idea is impossible when it is first born. The greatest ideas today are yet impossible. Possibility thinkers take great ideas and turn the impossibilities into possibilities. . . . The important issue is whether the idea is a good one. . . . If so, then develop a way to achieve what today is impossible. . . . Just because it's not possible today doesn't mean it can't be possible tomorrow. Our goals should always be based upon whether it would be a sensational thing to accomplish.

Commandment #4

Never reject a possibility because your mind is already made up!

I'm sure you've heard the saying, "Don't confuse me with the facts, my mind is already made up!" . . . People who never change their mind are either perfect or stubborn. I'm not perfect and neither are you. I'd rather change plans while still in port, than set sail and sink at sea.

Commandment #5

Never reject an idea because it's illegal!

Listen carefully, or you'll misinterpret this commandment. Some of the greatest ideas are impossible because they are illegal today. You never violate the law, but don't reject an idea because it's illegal. You probably have to change the law! . . .

Commandment #6

Never reject an idea because you don't have the money, manpower, muscle, or months to achieve it!

All it takes to accomplish the impossible is mind power, man power, money power, muscle power, and month power. If you don't have it, you can get it. . . . A super-successful person has very little resources except one thing — the capacity to take an idea and marshal stronger and smarter people around him to pull it off.

Commandment #7

Never reject an idea because it will create conflict!

The longer I've studied possibility thinking, the more I've come to one conclusion. You can never develop a possibility without creating problems. You can never establish a goal without generating a new set of tensions. You can never make a commitment without producing some conflict. Every idea worth anything is bound to have some people who don't go along with it.

Commandment #8

Never reject an idea because it's not your way of doing things!

Learn to accommodate. Prepare to expand. Plan to adjust. A different style, a new policy, a change in tradition — all are opportunities that need to be taken advantage of. Learn to compromise. Learn to be equilibristic. Maintain a balance between the tension of an opportunity that demands exploitation and the limitations of the resources available at the moment. . . .

Commandment #9

Never reject an idea because it might fail!

Every idea worth anything has failure potential within it. There is risk in everything. . . . Success is never certain, and failure is never final! . . . Success is never carved in granite. It is always molded in clay. . . .

Commandment #10

Never reject an idea because it's sure to succeed!

There are people today who back off if they are sure they will succeed. One reason is because these persons begin to imagine the ego fulfillment this success would give, and with an excuse of being humble, they pull out. . . . Only successful people can help people who are failing. . . . Just because an idea is going to be a success, don't be against it. . . .

Let's see where we are. If we are to become more productive, we must be more creative, and there are three things we can do to accomplish this.

1. Identify and remove mental obstacles that stifle creativity. Chapter 3 described these obstacles.
2. Adopt a set of positive and innovative attitudes. Dr. Schuller's Ten Commandments of Possibility Thinking, just presented, will help us do that.
3. Learn certain creative skills for use in productivity improvement activities, as described next.

CREATIVE SKILLS

We've all heard the remarks: "John's such a creative person, always thinking of something new" or "Linda is so innovative, just one clever idea after the other." But in fact, John and Linda probably are creative and innovative in only *certain* aspects of their lives. John may be a highly creative design engineer, with dozens of patents to his credit. But suggest to him some changes in the work flow of his engineering department, he will seize up and refuse to even discuss them. "After all," he'll say, "we've processed orders through engineering this way since I first came here, and it's worked OK in the past."

Similarly, Linda may be the best pediatric physician on the East Coast, recognized for her many technical innovations in the treatment of childhood diseases. But suggest to her some changes in the activities of the nursing stations in the hospital for which she is one of the directors, and she will seize up and answer, "Aren't you interested in the health of our patients in this hospital?"

In short, with few exceptions, our creativity is concentrated in certain areas of our lives, and is not easily transferred from one area to another. You may be the most creative artist, cabinet maker, landscape architect, design engineer, or heart surgeon in town. However, you probably are totally *uncreative* in other, vital areas of your life. In most business situations, this lack of creativity occurs in day-by-day work, right where we need to be *most* innovative if we are to become more productive.

Therefore, in all productivity improvement efforts, including your Operation Function Analysis program, we should become more creative in two ways: individually and as a group.

Individual Creativity

How can we become more creative as individuals? We've found that one of the best ways to do this is through *exercise*. Even though we are currently concerned with individual creativity, it works best if we do our exercises in a group. Why? We must learn to feel free to be *individually* creative in front of other people. Once we have achieved this skill, we then can be creative together as a group.

There are many creativity exercises. I've gathered them over the years, many from my former colleagues in General Electric, especially George Fridholm, value management consultant of Burnt Hills, New York. These exercises fall into two categories. First, there are problem sensitivity exercises, which test and improve our ability to *identify* and *define* the problem. Second, there are the creative solution exercises, which expand our ability to *solve* these problems. Here are several examples. Remember, work with your colleagues whenever possible. Remember, too, there is not necessarily just one right answer.

Problem Sensitivity Exercise No. 1. Listed below are three problems: start a fire; cut some cheese; lubricate a friction point. There are many tools you could use to help solve each of these three problems, depending on the definition, or exact nature of the problem in question. Some of these tools are listed next to each problem.

Describe how you might use each of the listed tools to help solve the associated problem.

Problem	*Tool*
Start a fire	1. A pen
	2. An onion
	3. A pocket watch
	4. A light bulb
	5. A bowling ball

Problem	*Tool*
Cut some cheese	1. A guitar
	2. A thermos bottle
	3. A hammer
	4. A pair of trousers
	5. A bed roll
Lubricate a friction point	1. Water
	2. A pencil
	3. A bottle of ink
	4. An eraser
	5. A dictionary

Problem Sensitivity Exercise No. 2. Look at Figure 4.1. How many squares can you see in this diagram? Take your time. Remember, your count will depend on how you define a square.

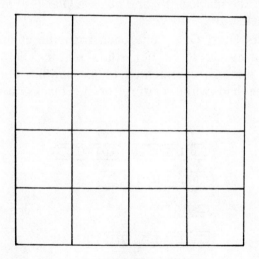

Figure 4.1

Problem Sensitivity Exercise No. 3. Years ago, a bunch of woodsmen had hauled their logs down to the main river, and now had to chain them together into a huge log raft to tow down the coast to a seaport where they would be loaded on a ship. As they proceeded to bind the logs together to form the raft, they suddenly realized they did not have a circular loop of chain, essential to the whole process.

Everything came to a halt, until finally the river boss located seven shorter pieces of chain. He asked the village blacksmith if he could join the pieces together to form the loop, and if so, how much would he charge.

The blacksmith said, "Surely," (blacksmiths always used proper adverbs back then) "be glad to. I'll have to cut a link at the end of each section of chain, and then forge it closed again to form the loop. Hm, that's a heavy chain. It'll be two dollars for each link I cut, and three dollars to forge it closed again. Seven lengths, times five bucks, that'll be thirty-five dollars for the whole job. Have one of your men bring the chain and the money, and I'll do the job right away."

The river boss went back to his logging area and gathered up the seven lengths of chain, as shown in Figure 4.2. He instructed Olaf, a young lad just off the boat from the old country, to haul the pieces of chain up to the blacksmith, and he gave Olaf the thirty-five dollars to pay the blacksmith.

A few hours later, Olaf came back with the chain, now formed into the continuous loop. For some reason Olaf seemed quite pleased with himself, commented to his buddies about the dandy little lunch he had while waiting for the blacksmith to make the

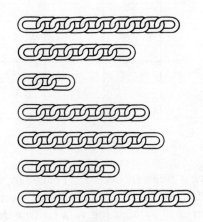

Figure 4.2

loop, and was contently puffing away on a good cigar, several more of which he gave to his closest friends.

Why was Olaf so content? Where did he get the money for his lunch and cigars? What did he know, what problem sensitivity skills did he have that neither the river boss nor the blacksmith had? Or did the blacksmith learn these skills too? After all, he was seen smoking a good cigar later that day!

Problem Sensitivity Exercise No. 4. Remember, identify and define the problem before you try to solve it.

1. If you went to bed at eight o'clock at night, and set the alarm to get up at nine in the morning, how many hours of sleep would you get?
2. Do they have a fourth of July in England?
3. If you had only one match and entered a room where there was an oil lamp, an oil heater, and a gas heater, which would you light first?
4. If a doctor gave you three pills and told you take one every half-hour, how long would they last?
5. Some months have thirty days and some months have thirty-one. How many have twenty-eight days?
6. How many players does each baseball team have on the field? How many outs in an inning?
7. A farmer had seventeen sheep. All but nine died. How many were left?
8. Divide ½ into 30 and add 10. What's the answer?
9. An antique dealer in Peoria, Illinois, opened his shop on Sunday and sold some ancient Roman coins marked 56 B.C. with the likeness of Caesar Aurelius on one side, and a laurel wreath on the other. Shortly after that, he was arrested by the police. Why?
10. How many animals of each sex did Noah take aboard the ark with him?

Creative Solution Exercises. As mentioned before, there are two categories of creativity exercises: problem sensitivity and creative solution. Let's look at some examples of creative solution exercises.

Get some paper, write your answers as you go, and zip right along. Spend only one or two minutes on each exercise.

1. List all the improvements you would like to see in an ordinary office telephone.
2. List all the things wrong with our national election processes.
3. List all the words you can think of beginning with the letter *E.*
4. List synonyms for the word *dark.*
5. Make several four-word sentences. In each sentence, start the first word with the letter *W,* the second word with *c,* the third with *e,* and the fourth with *n.* (*Example:* We congregate every noon.) Use a given word only once.
6. List as many uses as you can think of for a brick in addition to the traditional construction use.
7. The design in Figure 4.3 can be made from seventeen matches. Take away four of the matches so as to leave three squares and nothing more.
8. List all the titles you can for the following plot of a short story:

    A missionary has been captured by cannibals in the jungle. He is in the pot, and is about to be boiled, when a princess of the tribe obtains a promise for his release if he will become her mate. He refuses and is boiled to death.

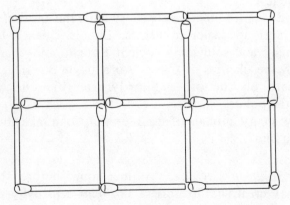

Figure 4.3

9. Using idea-spurring approaches — adapt, modify, magnify, minify, substitute, rearrange, reverse, combine — and list things that can be made from an average American automobile, *other* than a means of transportation.
10. If the function of a pencil is to make marks, list as many different ways as you can think of to use it to make marks.

Group Creativity

Let's recap where we are. In the preceding chapter, we read that real productivity improvement requires change, and that change in turn requires creativity and innovation. To achieve this, we first must recognize and remove the mental obstacles that stifle our creative potential.

In the first part of this chapter, we learned that we also should develop positive, creative attitudes and skills. These creative skills take two forms: Individual creativity and group creativity. We have discussed individual creativity. Now let's move on to group creativity.

Group innovation is new to many in this country. Indeed, many still are convinced that it just won't work, and this attitude is a major obstacle to real improvement, as described in the preceding chapter.

Why is there this resistance to group innovation? For centuries, most formal meetings in the Western world have been largely adversarial, in which one side tries to outmaneuver the other. This is true in government parliaments and legislatures, in religious conclaves, in labor-management meetings, in our courts of law, etc. With these as role models, it is easy to see why many of our day-by-day meetings in our work take on an equally adversarial overtone. Since innovation and creativity can hardly flourish in such an adversarial environment, many of us have come to believe that group creativity is impossible.

Some years ago, a new approach was fostered, brainstorming, and became all the rage. Before long, everyone was doing it, but often without really knowing how to do it. A bunch of people would sit down in a room, and everyone would begin to shout out their ideas. Naturally, it did not work well, and as with many fads, it gained a bad name.

However, new forms of group innovation are much more than the old brainstorming, and as a result they work more effectively. Organizations that have used O.F.A. have found that the success of group innovation is greatly enhanced if you do two things.

First, clearly establish the roles of everyone involved in a group session, that is:

- Have one person act as the session leader. Each time your O.F.A. team, employee circle, or working group meets to innovate and develop new ideas, one member should act as the session leader. *Note:* This is *not* the same as the facilitator role that has gained recent popularity. The session leader is a regular member of the group, who just happens to serve as the leader at this time because of his special skill or knowledge of the subject under discussion. At the next meeting, a different person might serve as session leader.
- Have the other members of the group act as active session participants, with specific responsibilities for generating ideas.

Second, establish a set of guidelines for both the session leader and the participants, sort of a "Robert's Rules of Order" for group innovation. Here are some rules we have found helpful for the session leader.

Rules for Session Leader

Be a leader, not a lecturer. The prime job of the leader is to draw out ideas from the other group members, and to lead the group along a constructive path. Even though you may know more about the subject than anyone else in the group, do not stand up and lecture the group. That will kill any hope of real innovation.

Be positive. Maintain the role of a positive leader. When another group member presents an idea, agree with him. Even if you cannot agree with every detail of his idea, at least agree with his right and responsibility to present the idea. Avoid arguments, controversies, and evaluations, for they will stifle further ideas. Even the slightest sign of uncertainty or disapproval by the group leader can have a smothering effect.

Stay off the defensive. It is not unusual for participants in the session to attack the session leader. They may criticize his organization, or his work and role within the organization. This is especially true during the first few meetings of the group, until you can defuse the adversarial spirit so common in our daily lives. The session leader should swallow these attacks, stay off the defensive, and guide the meeting back to the principal subject.

Guide the discussion. The group leader should state the subject of the working session, and ensure that the group stays on that subject. This may sound obvious, but one of the main weaknesses of the old brainstorming sessions was that they wandered all over the place. If the leader of a group creativity session senses the group is drifting off to another subject, he should state this, establish a time and place for a meeting on this new subject, and then return the current meeting to the original subject.

Restate ideas. Often a group member will present an idea in a rambling, even disorganized manner. This is all right. The important thing is to get the idea out. The group leader then can help by restating the idea in clearer terms, acceptable, of course, to the original speaker, and recording the idea on a blackboard or easel for all to see.

Ask questions. When a group member presents an idea, you as group leader should ask questions to encourage both the speaker and others to continue with that thought train. Avoid pontificating or making authoritarian statements and evaluations, even though you may know a lot about the subject. If you do this, others will clam up, and you will lose your meeting. Remember, your job is to draw out ideas from the other group members.

Develop one idea at a time. When a group member presents an idea, focus on it, expand and develop it. Almost immediately, however, other ideas will pop up. The session leader should record these on a separate board or easel for later consideration by the group, and should not allow the group to deflect the discussion from the first idea until the group's input on that idea dries up naturally.

Then the session leader can go back and pick up one of the other ideas for development.

Revitalize thoughts with positive contributions. At times the creative session will lag. Group members will run out of gas. As the session leader, be ready to make positive contributions to revitalize thoughts and get things going again. Recognize relationships, summarize, restate ideas, etc.

Adjourn the session. When additional facts are needed or ideas must be tested, then adjourn the meeting. Don't keep the meeting going just to "fill out the hour"!

Rules for Session Participants

Each participant in the creativity session should observe certain rules if the group is to succeed in its work. Here are five good ones.

Present your ideas in a positive manner. Too often we hear a group participant say to others, "Why can't we cut the proposal processing cycle time by at least twenty percent?" or, "Why can't we improve the quality of that weld so customers will be more satisfied?"

When a person presents an idea this way, he is asking for defeat and rejection. He literally is asking his fellow participants to tell him why his idea is no good and will not work! Of course they will cooperate. They will give him ten or twenty such reasons for failure, ample justification for the speaker to discard his idea and retreat into his shell.

It is much more effective to say, "In what way can we reduce the proposal processing cycle time by at least twenty percent?" With this approach, the speaker asks for positive contributions, and the discussion moves ahead in a constructive manner.

Criticism is ruled out. During a group innovation session, the participants should withhold all adverse judgment. New ideas are too fragile to take the heat of immediate question and rejection. If a group member has doubts, he may note them for later consideration, but should not bring them up now.

Free-wheeling is welcome. The wilder, more audacious the idea, the more acceptable it is. It is much easier to tame down a big idea, then to try to puff up a small one, as described earlier.

Quantity is wanted. The greater the number of ideas, the more chance of getting useful ones. Once the ideas are flowing in a group creativity session, let them run. Later, you can harvest the best for final evaluation and recommendation.

Talk with any great inventor or scientist, and ask how he conceived of that one great idea for which he is famous. Chances are high he will answer, "Oh, I thought of thousands of ideas on the subject and threw away all but this one!"

Combine and improve on ideas of others. Contribute your own ideas, improve the ideas of others in the group. Combine several ideas into one new idea. Don't worry about the origin of the idea. Someone wrote, "Almost anything is possible if you don't worry about who will get the credit."

Group innovation is strong medicine. It is new to many people in our country, and goes against the grain of all we have learned since childhood about the value of the individual mind, and the role of the lonely inventor.

However, group innovation does work, and can bring solid benefits, especially if you follow rules such as those presented here.

SUMMARY

Recently an officer of a major bank proclaimed that the single most important element of a successful productivity improvement program was a detailed, comprehensive measurement system. He was wrong, and I told him so. Significant though measurement is, the most important ingredient of any improvement program really is creativity, at all levels of the organization, from the most senior executive down through the workers in the offices and factories. Hence, everyone of us involved in productivity improvement must:

- Remove the mental obstacles that limit our creative potential
- Cultivate positive, creative attitudes
- Learn innovative skills, both as individuals and as groups
- Apply our new found innovative attitudes and skills to our productivity improvement programs.

Chapter 5
Demands Drive the Business

In Chapters 2, 3, and 4, you read about some of the *human* factors in the logic of O.F.A., that is, the need to:

- Do it yourself, through broad participation by people involved in the organization
- Recognize and remove mental obstacles to creative thinking
- Develop really creative attitudes and skills, and use them to gain major productivity improvements.

There is more to the O.F.A. logic than this, however. Chapters 5, 6, and 7 will present some of the *technical* factors in the O.F.A. logic which will help you analyze and improve the activities in your organization. The current chapter focuses on the first of these factors, demand identification, analysis, and modification.

The principal challenge in improving productivity is to eliminate unnecessary work, not just speed it up. Sounds great — but how?

Demands are the key. Each organization is hit and driven by demands placed on it by other organizations, as illustrated in Figure 5.1. People in the organization perform work functions to meet these demands, and while doing this also place downstream demands on still other groups.

This leads us to the third rule of productivity improvement in the professional, knowledge, office area:

Rule 3: The productivity of an organization is determined by the characteristics of the demands placed on it — more than by any other factor.

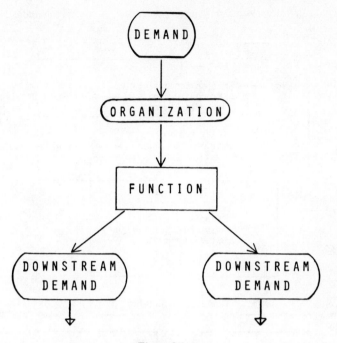

Figure 5.1

For example, customer orders enter the order handling department, which performs work functions such as order editing, order entry, order monitoring, order control, etc. As a result of performing these functions, this department also places production orders on downstream organizations such as design engineering, materials management, credit and collections, etc., which lead them to do their work.

If the incoming customer orders are off schedule, inaccurate, incomplete, or sent to the wrong place, then unnecessary work results, and the productivity of the order handling department suffers. Furthermore, the subsequent downstream demands often will have these same characteristics, spreading unnecessary work and low productivity throughout the whole organization.

THE DEMAND-FUNCTION NETWORK

The activities of any business, service, or government organization are composed of dozens, perhaps hundreds of such demands and

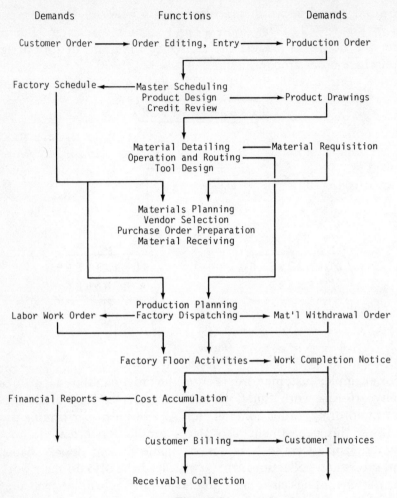

Figure 5.2

functions. A partial list for a typical equipment manufacturer might include:

Demands	*Functions*
Customer orders	Order editing and entry
Production orders	Master scheduling
Factory schedules	Product design
Product drawings	Credit review
Material requisitions	Material detailing

However, this is more than a list — it is a network, as shown partially in Figure 5.2. (The figure is only a simplified view. For instance, the networks leading off from the functions of tool design and purchase order preparation are not shown.)

Notice, this is *not* the same as the detailed operational flow diagram long used in industrial engineering studies. This new network focuses on major functions and the demands that drive them. The activities of any organization can be expressed by such a network of demands and functions. Once you have done this for your own organization — and really understand this network — you are ready to start after the big gains. How?

PRODUCTIVITY IMPROVEMENT THROUGH DEMAND MODIFICATION

Rule 3 on page 46 tells us that the nature of the demands determine the productivity of the business. If this is so, and it is, then the best way to get major improvements is to *change* the demands. We can do this through four simple steps:

1. Identify the unnecessary work in each function
2. Identify the demand that drives each function, and the characteristics or features of that demand that cause the unnecessary work
3. Modify and simplify the demand, removing the offending features so as to eliminate the unnecessary work
4. Change the work flow to meet the new, simplified demand, and gain lasting structural improvements.

On the surface, this approach to demand identification and modification may seem obvious and simplistic. You may wonder, "Why bring that up?" Here's why.

In the past, and even now, work simplification experts — industrial engineers, computer system designers, operation auditors — have too often ignored the impact of demands. Instead, they concentrate on the details of work flow, seeking to speed up these activities. In the process, they speed up both the necessary *and* unnecessary work. This is wrong, since unnecessary work performed rapidly and "efficiently" is still just that — unnecessary work.

Example. Every business manager receives scores of totally unnecessary letters from colleagues in his own business. Recently, as a result of new, efficient word processing equipment and systems and computer electronic mail, he can now receive even more unnecessary and unwanted mail.

Example. New material and production planning systems permit us to easily modify our material acquisition and factory schedules with lightning speed. Sounds great. However, this often only results in "nervous" production control systems that thrash about in response to every tremor in the order forecast.

DEMAND IDENTIFICATION

In order to modify demands, we must first identify them. Often they are not as obvious and clearly defined as they may seem.

To illustrate, the word *demand* has a number of general meanings. Here's a list of one class of demands:

1. Keep the inventory storage area in the field warehouse locked up securely to prevent unauthorized removals
2. Don't spill coffee on the vice president's new rug
3. Treat your employees fairly
4. Get to work before 8:30 A.M.
5. Keep the assembly area free from rejected defective parts; dispose of them properly.

Now these are all good demands, but they are not O.F.A. demands. As we saw before, an O.F.A. demand is an event or transaction that causes work to be done, that is, causes people in an organization to perform functions.

There *could* be an O.F.A. demand associated with each situation mentioned above, as listed below:

1. An *inventory withdrawal order,* presented to the inventory attendant, for the requested items
2. A *cleaning work order,* issued by the vice president's secretary to the office maintenance foreman, requesting special cleaning services

3. A third level grievance *request for arbitration* under the
    union contract, prepared by the employee and union steward
    and presented to the manager of union relations
4. A *weekly attendance record,* prepared by a design engineer
    and submitted to the manager of engineering administration
5. *Scrap ticket,* prepared by the assembly foreman, showing the
    reason for scrap and area of disposition.

In summary, an O.F.A. demand is an event or transaction initiated
by a person or group, and causing someone to perform a work
function.

Typical Demands

Here is a list of typical O.F.A. demands in an equipment manufacturing business:

Customer inquiry
Request for quotation
Request for engineering data
Price analysis sheet
Request for proposal drawing
Handwritten proposal spec.
Customer order – mail
Customer order – TWX/phone
Memorandum booking order
Order entry info. sheet
Change order to engineering
Approval tracing
Certified tracing
Request for shipping date
Engineering release to mfg.
Vendor quotation
Vendor invoice
Material rejection notice
Engineering parts list
Engineering assembly list
Order pricing data sheet

Purchase requisition
Purchase order
Shipping order – handwritten
Shipping order – typed
Credit approval request
Engineering info. sheet
Engineering sketch
Customer approval drawings
Key punch form
Engineering change notice
Request for routing
Process sheet
Manufacturing drawing
Floor documentation
Purchase order shortage list
Stores shortage list
Open order report
Late order report
Daily transaction report
Stock status report
Order monitoring data sheet

Now take a few minutes and make a list of typical demands that pass through your own organization. If you work in an insurance company, think of some of the demands associated with portfolio management. If in a hospital, think of demands at a surgical ward nursing station. If in a shipping company, think of the demands involved in overhauling and supplying a tanker.

TYPES OF O.F.A. DEMANDS

There are several types of O.F.A. demands, and if you understand them, you can more effectively identify them.

Documented Versus Implied Demands

There are documented versus implied demands. All the demands on the preceding list are documented demands. You can pick up, hold in your hand, and read a customer inquiry or a material rejection notice.

However, many demands are implied — such as a *requirement* for a weekly attendance report, or a *requirement* for a monthly budget reconciliation report. No paper document or other record requests the monthly budget report. The budget analyst just knows that the report must be prepared. Nevertheless, the implied demand is just as much a demand as the customer inquiry.

In fact, implied demands often are more critical than documented ones. Since they are *not* documented, they are less well defined, harder to identify, more susceptible to misinterpretation, and more likely to cause unnecessary work. Search for them.

External Versus Internal Demands

Two other important types of O.F.A. demands are external and internal demands. Referring back to the list of demands, we find:

> External demands: Customer inquiry
> Memorandum booking order
> Customer order — mail
>
> Internal demands: Price analysis sheet
> Certified drawing
> Material rejection notice

Experience indicates that at least 80–90% of all demands handled by most businesses are internal demands, hence are especially available for modification.

As cases will show later, even the external demands often can be modified. In fact, since the external demands often are at the head end of the entire work flow process, any improvements you make in one of them can have tremendous leverage, and result in beneficial impacts throughout the downstream organizations.

One manufacturing company, for example, often accepted customer orders with incomplete information. In order to meet shipping requirements, they released these orders for processing on the basis of assumed specifications, a common practice in many equipment manufacturing businesses.

Later, when the missing information was received, they made changes "on the fly" to the orders then in process. This often resulted in special expediting and handling, rescheduling, broken production runs, scrap and rework, etc.

In fact, during one period, 32 changes were submitted by customers for orders in process, but these changes exploded through the downstream organizations and resulted in over 2,500 individual changes in engineering design details and factory floor processing.

That is, 32 changes in external demands resulted in over 2,500 changes in related internal demands. That's leverage. It was obvious to everyone involved that even modest improvements in the completeness and timeliness of these incoming orders would enable the business to better serve its customers, control internal costs, and meet shipping schedules. On this basis, company management approached the customers and worked with them to improve the completeness and timeliness of these orders. (See the case history given in Chapter 17 for more on this.)

So remember to go after those external demands. They can be hard to modify, but they exert great leverage, and changes you make to them can bring benefits throughout the organization.

Interdepartmental Demands

Internal demands may also be interdepartmental demands, that is, demands that pass through the interfaces between departments of the total organization, and connect the work performed in one department with work performed in others. Such demands can be

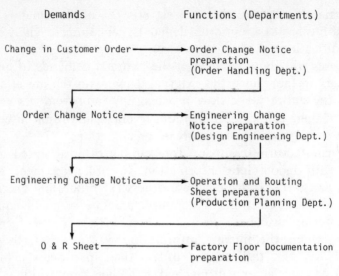

Figure 5.3

especially challenging because the people within the department
often may view these interdepartmental demands as *external* demands,
with all the problems and opportunities described before.

We have all heard comments such as this one, made by a buyer in
the purchasing department:

> Sure. I know that special material requisitions from design engi-
> neering always take four times as long to process as the regular
> ones, but we can't do anything about that. I talked to Joe Barota
> about this — you know, the manager of the drafting office — and
> he said that was the way the system worked. So I never bothered
> to say anything more to anyone after that. Anyway, it's their job
> to handle that.

Figure 5.3 illustrates these interdepartmental demands and shows
how an external demand — a change in a customer order — can
trigger off a network of internal demands and functions, bouncing
from one department to another, often imbedded within an integrated
computer system such as CAD/CAM (computer aided design/computer
aided manufacturing).

Now check yourself to be sure you understand what we've just
discussed. Review your own organization, and then fill in the lines

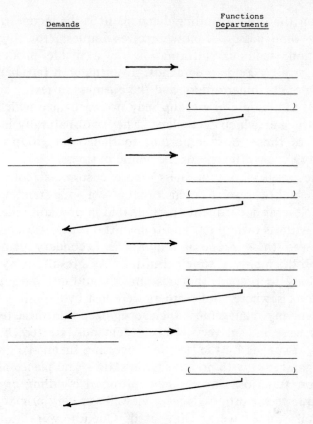

Figure 5.4

on Figure 5.4 with typical interorganizational demands, the functions performed to meet these demands, and the different organizations which perform the demands.

Primary Versus Secondary Demands

Two other types of demands often encountered are primary and secondary demands. Every organization is first established to handle certain primary demands. However, as time passes, it picks up a number of secondary demands. Two things frequently happen.

First, the people in the department can become so overwhelmed by the ever increasing volume of secondary demands that they neglect the original, primary demands. For example, the primary demand on the order handling department is the incoming customer order. As time passes, it now receives requests for shipping date confirmation, technical information on available products, plant tours, etc. — all secondary demands. Eventually, it falls behind on its processing of customer orders, and the business suffers.

Second, the people in a group may not recognize which demands are primary and which secondary. They will naturally identify the primaries as those most important to their own group's activities, which may *not* be primary for the whole business.

This occurred in one business whose customers required formal proposals before placing their orders — a long-standing industry practice. Several departments participated in preparing these proposals, each with its own queue and transmittal time. Also, each department viewed these proposal requests as secondary demands, and worked on them only as time permitted. As a result, many proposals took so long to prepare that customers could not wait, and placed their orders elsewhere. Solid orders were lost by default.

The company management then recognized that these requests for proposals were indeed very primary demands, treated, however, as secondary demands by the people processing them. To correct this, they reorganized — with no increase in staff — and placed all proposal preparation functions in one new proposal handling organization, where requests for proposals were viewed as a very primary demand. Transmittal times were eliminated. Queues were substantially reduced. Now 90% of all proposals are processed within three days, proposal quality has improved, and many orders previously lost are now obtained. That's productivity improvement!

Watch for primary and secondary demands, identify and treat them properly from the viewpoint of the total business.

Take a minute now for review. List a dozen or so demands that have passed into your organization this last week. How many of them are primary, how many secondary? Are they primary and secondary to your department, or to the whole organization?

Self-Imposed Demands

One more important type of demand remains: those which are self-imposed. Every organization is hit by many demands. Most of them are legitimate and necessary. Nevertheless, we often see demands we create and impose on ourselves. Some of these self-imposed demands might have been legitimate years ago, but now are no longer needed, yet are kept by habit.

For example, the inside sales department receives the customer orders and processes them to design engineering, where drawings and bills of material are created and released to manufacturing.

However, the superintendent of the final assembly department, and the foreman of final inspection — even though they both receive copies of all necessary drawings and bills of material — insist on receiving copies of the original customer orders. As a result, they must perform several functions on these customer orders: file, review, update for changes, etc., all of which is unnecessary and unproductive work.

Why do they insist on placing this demand on themselves? Because years ago assembly bills were not issued; the customer order was the sole source of information on the complete product. Also, people in the assembly and inspection areas want to keep up with the customer orders.

Self-imposed demands are a common cause of unnecessary and unproductive work. Look for them. Remove them.

SUMMARY

Every organization is a network of demands and related work functions. The characteristics of the demands that impact an organization determine its productivity. Therefore, demand identification and modification is a major key to reduction of unnecessary work and productivity improvement.

Demands at the head end of the work flow exert leverage, and their improvement often benefits many downstream departments. Learn to recognize different types of demands because each type presents a unique challenge and opportunity.

Chapter 6
Functions and Operations —
The Building Blocks

Work flow in an organization can be analyzed at three general levels of detail: elemental motions, operations, and functions.

In their time and motion studies, industrial engineers often are concerned with elemental motions. (*Examples:* reach for folder and grasp; pick up two pages, position and staple; feed one hundred envelopes into opening machine.) Although there is a place for elemental motion analysis in clerical work simplification, it has little role in productivity improvement in the knowledge worker areas, hence is not involved in Operation Function Analysis.

In O.F.A. we are concerned with both functions and operations. In a typical manufacturing or distribution business, you will identify one to two hundred major functions, made up of literally thousands of operations. This chapter will describe the role of these functions and operations in O.F.A.

OPERATIONS – THE SMALL BLOCKS

An operation is the basic work unit and the lowest level of detail used in Operation Function Analysis. Each operation is composed of dozens, perhaps hundreds of elemental motions, all too small to be considered individually in knowledge work productivity improvement.

Each operation is driven by a single demand, and occurs within one department of the business. People normally view their own work in terms of operations. Examples of the operations are shown in Table 6.1.

A clear knowledge of operations in your business will permit you to:

- Recognize the alternate routes through which the demands travel
- Recognize the business activities that consume large amounts of resources, i.e., effort, expense, and cycle time

Table 6.1. Operations and Driving Demands.

OPERATION	DRIVING DEMAND	ORGANIZATION PERFORMING OPERATION
Compare order pricing with quotation	Customer order	Inside sales
Compare technical features on order with proposal	Customer order	Application engineering
Confirm requested shipping date	Customer order	Production planning
Prepare engineering change notice	Product design change	Design engineering
Review E.C.N.'s and evaluate impact on final inspection needs	E.C.N.	Factory inspection
Prepare inspection rejection and disposition notice	Rejected part	Factory inspection
Prepare manual purchase order	Special material requisition	Purchasing
Inspect vendor shipment when received	Receiving inspection request	Receiving department
Prepare promotional packet	Letter from interested party	Sales promotion

- Relate the work performed with the people who do it
- Gain a better understanding of your organization's activities.

Take time now to test yourself to make sure you understand operations. Make a list of a dozen or so operations which occur in your business, the driving demand which causes people to perform each operation, and the department or group within your business that performs the operation.

FUNCTIONS — THE BIG BLOCKS

A function is a group of related operations performed to meet a single demand. Every organization is unique and has its own set of functions, and they are best defined by example.

Functions in Equipment Manufacturing Business

Here is a list of functions identified by the management of a manufacturer of cranes and hoists. Notice they divided their functions into three main categories.

- *Preliminary processes:* those functions that are future oriented, get the organization ready to handle the subsequent main-line activities
- *Main-line processes:* those functions that get the order, receive it, convey it through engineering and manufacturing, ship it to the customer, supply the service parts, and the financial functions associated with these main-line activities
- *Supporting processes:* those functions carried on to permit the main-line processes to be conducted, although not a part of the main line activities themselves

Functions in the Preliminary Processes

General business planning
Market forecasting
Product planning and development
Sales development
Resource planning and development
Financial forecasting
Financial planning and development
Manufacturing standards development
Manufacturing facilities development
Price policy administration
Gross margin analysis
Price book administration

Functions in the Main-Line Processes

Getting the order
Sales liaison
Direct selling
Product application engineering
Cost estimating
Proposal preparation

Order editing
Order entry
Order acknowledgment
Order followup
Order control
Order monitoring

Designing the product
Advance engineering
Design scheduling
Standard design engineering
Engineering change notice initiation
Engineering documentation
Engineering liaison

Planning the manufacturing process
Manufacturing specification preparation
Manufacturing specification processing
Manufacturing documentation distribution
Manufacturing documentation interpretation
Engineering change notice processing
Manufacturing master scheduling
Manufacturing process planning
Parts routes planning
Parts routes timing
Direct labor planning
Nondurable tools stocking and issuance

Acquiring and stocking the material for manufacturing
Inventory control
Vendor evaluation and selection
Purchase order processing
Purchase order monitoring and expediting
Vendor invoice processing
Material receiving
Receiving inspection
Stock control: raw materials
Stock control: components
Stock control: finished goods

Manufacturing the product
Factory loading and scheduling
Factory order release
Direct labor dispatching to factory floor
Work movement between work stations in factory
In-process inspection: welding
In-process inspection: machining
In-process inspection: assembly
Inspection documentation
Disposition of nonconforming materials
Shipping: domestic
Shipping: export
Timekeeping and labor reporting
Expediting: due to late release of order
Expediting: due to modification of specifications
Expediting: due to misplaced materials
Expediting: due to misplaced documentation
Expediting: due to in-process material rejections
Expediting: due to inventory records error
Expediting: miscellaneous

Servicing the product
Parts catalog preparation
Replacement parts sales
Service and warranty administration

Administration, accounting, and collecting for order
Order closeout
Customer invoicing
Credit and collections
Cost accumulation and accounting
Cost analysis and control
General supervision
General clerical

Functions in the Supporting Processes

Liaison with outside inspectors
Employee training

> Employee relations
> Union relations
> Technical assistance
> Facilities maintenance
> Machine repair and overhaul
> Industrial engineering monitoring and review
> Information systems planning and development
> Computer operations
> Return goods processing

Functions in a Hospital

This functional approach is applicable over a wide variety of organizations. For example, in a medium-size, non-teaching hospital, the functions might fall into the following categories:

General Nursing Services

These include all activities associated with the direct contact, general treatment and care of patients in the hospital wards. *Examples:* Administration of general medicines, routine medical monitoring and observation of patients, patient comfort care, etc.

Special Patient Services

These are specialized services provided patients above and beyond the general nursing services. *Examples:* Outpatient services, surgical services, anesthesia services, radiation therapy, respiratory therapy, etc.

General Support Services

These are the activities needed to carry out the "hotel" aspects of the hospital. *Examples:* Laundry and housekeeping, food services, maintenance and engineering, purchasing, security and safety, etc.

Patient Records and General Accounting

These are the general record-keeping activities of the hospital. *Examples:* Patient admission and release, cost accounting, general accounting, claims processing, information systems development, etc.

Human Resources

These activities are associated with the hospital employees. *Examples:* Hiring and releasing of employees, employee training and development, employee productivity programs, etc.

Characteristic of Functions

In any case, regardless of the type of organization involved, a function is a major unit of work with the following general characteristics:

Driven by a Demand

A function is performed to meet a single driving demand. To illustrate this, here are a few functions from the list for the crane and hoist manufacturer, and the related driving demands.

Function	*Driving Demand*
Order editing	Customer order
Advance engineering	Production order
E.C.N. initiation	Design change request
E.C.N. processing	Engineering change notice
Parts route planning	Engineering change notice
Purchase order expediting	Late purchase order

If it appears that a single function is driven by more than one demand, the function probably is too broad and should be divided until the relationship of one demand to one function is achieved. However, a single demand often drives more than one function, as illustrated above. The engineering change notice drives both E.C.N. processing and parts route planning. That is, whenever an E.C.N. is issued by design engineering, many other organizations perform a number of operations, all involved in general E.C.N. processing. In addition, this same E.C.N. causes the manufacturing engineering organization to plan new routings for all parts affected by the E.C.N.

Composed of Operations

A function is composed of a number of operations — five, ten, fifteen or more. A dozen is typical. To illustrate, take the function of order editing. In one company is was made up of eleven operations, each

Table 6.2. Operations That Comprise Order Editing.

OPERATION NUMBER	OPERATION DESCRIPTION	MAN-HOURS PER MONTH
1	Review order; complete order work sheet	160
2	Compare technical features of order with proposal	220
3	Compare order pricing and quotation	240
4	Check customer shipping arrangements	130
5	Confirm requested shipping date	90
6	Check commission distributions	80
7	Check credit classification	160
8	Refer exceptions to credit office	70
9	Check customer coding	40
10	Prepare field sales question form and send to field sales office	120
11	Prepare order summary sheets and job folder	230
	Total time devoted to function of order editing	1,540

consuming the effort shown in Table 6.2, with a total of 1,540 man-hours per month for the function.

Spans Organizations

A function often spans two or more organizations. For example, in order editing, the distribution is shown in Table 6.3. Although the inside sales organization performs the majority of the operations involved in order editing, four other organizations contribute significantly: design engineering, traffic, production planning, and credit and collection.

Table 6.3. Organizations Involved in Order Editing.

OPERATION NUMBER	PERFORMING ORGANIZATION
1	Inside sales
2	Design engineering
3	Inside sales
4	Traffic department
5	Production planning
6	Inside sales
7	Inside sales
8	Credit and collection
9	Inside sales
10	Inside sales
11	Inside sales

Let's test ourselves again, and make sure we understand the relationships between driving demands, functions, operations, and the groups which perform this work. Table 6.4 illustrates this. Review it, and then fill in a couple of examples from your own organization.

FUNCTIONS AND OPERATIONS — WHY BOTH?

For years, work simplification and general efficiency programs focused on operations, even elemental motions. Why are we suddenly introducing the concept of *function?*

Identifiable, Repetitive, Measurable

For purposes of productivity improvement, the activities of any organization should be divided into units of work that are identifiable, generally repetitive, and consistently measurable.

For example, in clerical work individuals perform the same operations, generally in a fixed sequence, every day, every week, every month. Therefore, productivity improvement focuses on these *individuals* and their *operations.*

On the other hand, conditions are very different in the professional, knowledge, office worker areas. A person does *not* perform a sequence of repetitive operations. Few if any people perform the same operations. Although operations may be identifiable, they are not repetitive nor consistently measurable. Also, knowledge work activities are much more complex than clerical work. Closely related work often is performed in several different areas throughout the business, as in the order editing example given earlier.

Because functions are larger, broader units of work, they tend to repeat, are consistently measurable, and are able to span two or more groups. Therefore, in professional knowledge work activities, productivity improvement works best when focused on the *group,* and the *functions* it performs.

Since O.F.A. is applicable throughout the whole business, it addresses a mixture of both clerical and knowledge work activities. Therefore, it uses both operations and functions.

Functions Improve Communications

Perhaps the greatest reason to use both operations and functions is to improve communications. Many people who are involved in the

Table 6.4. Demands, Functions, Operations in Your Organization.

DEMAND	FUNCTION	OPERATIONS	PERFORMING ORGANIZATIONS
Customer order	Order editing	Review order, complete order work sheet	Inside Sales
		Compare technical features of order	Design Eng'g.
		Compare order pricing and quotation	Inside Sales
		Check customer shipping arrangements	Traffic Dept.
		Confirm requested shipping date	Prod. Planning
		etc.	etc.

day-by-day conduct of the business view their own work in terms of operations. Therefore, as described in Chapter 9, you will usually collect information on knowledge work activities on the basis of operations.

Senior managers think in terms of broader functions, functions that may span several departments. Therefore, as described in Chapters 11 and 12, you will evaluate the results of your productivity improvement work, and present your recommendations in terms of functions.

This distinction between operations and functions is important in communications, as illustrated by the following example from a light manufacturing business.

Example of Improved Communications

For months, people in the production planning and control organization had urged their division general manager to invest in a new material and production planning system. To support their case, they had described how much time they devoted to each operation in the current process, and how they could save several hours here, several more there, etc. The general manager was unimpressed by these details, and remained unconvinced.

Using the methods described in Chapter 10 and 11, they condensed their detailed data, expressed it in terms of functions, and determined the following:

Function	*Man-hrs/month*
Production planning and scheduling	770
Hot listing and expediting	3,480

In other words, the "bottom-up" function of hot listing and expediting exceeded the "top down" function of production planning and scheduling by a ratio of 4.5 : 1, clearly a totally unacceptable condition. The division general manager immediately recognized the depth of his production planning and control problems, and established a program to improve the material and production planning process. (See the case study in Chapter 16.)

When the production planning specialists expressed their data in terms of functions, they accomplished to things:

1. They presented their case in the language their general manager understood – functions.
2. They talked numbers big and dramatic enough to command the attention of their general manager.

THE O.F.A. RATIO – A BASIC PERFORMANCE MEASURE

There are many approaches to measurement of productivity, but they generally fall into three broad categories:

1. *Overall business measurements,* perhaps even tied into total corporate financial statements. Important though these may be for corporate productivity planning, they are of little use to the operating manager.
2. *Functional measurements.* These measure the effectiveness of the day-by-day business activities, and enable the operating manager to evaluate specific productivity trends.
3. *Detailed measurements* based on operations or even elemental motions. As indicated earlier, these are of value in some forms of industrial engineering studies, but are of little use to the operating manager in professional, knowledge work productivity improvement.

The O.F.A. ratio is in the second category. As a basic performance measure, it should be a part of every improvement program. Figure 6.1 illustrates the calculation of this O.F.A. ratio. In the preceding example, 1,540 man-hours a month were devoted to the function of order editing for 120 orders a month. On this basis, the O.F.A. Ratio for the function of order editing is 12.8 man-hours per order.

This O.F.A. ratio can be used for many things:

- To identify high effort functions
- To evaluate variations in productivity over a period of time
- To compare effort required to process similar demands in different organizations
- To compare effort required for similar demands passing through different routes within the same organization.

One key point. The O.F.A. ratio is *not* the same as a burden allocation ratio broadly used in some productivity measurement approaches, for one main reason. The denominator of the O.F.A.

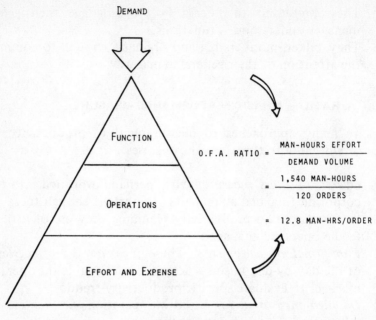

Figure 6.1

ratio is, in fact, the *driving* demand for that function, not just some convenient, statistically related variable.

Another key point. O.F.A. ratios are *not* the same as the predetermined labor factors that have been developed and used by some consulting firms as a basis for indirect labor planning and measurement. Details of the calculation and use of O.F.A. ratios are given in Chapters 10 and 11.

SUMMARY

The work flow in the professional, knowledge, office activities of an organization is composed of a relatively small number of major functions, each in turn composed of many smaller operations.

In O.F.A., we collect information on these activities in terms of operations — the language of the analyst — and we evaluate and present our recommendations in terms of functions — the language of the manager.

The O.F.A. ratio is a basic performance measure, especially useful in the knowledge work areas because it permits operating managers to evaluate productivity trends on the basis of broad business functions.

Chapter 7
Interorganizational Work
Flow — The Big Purse

Hear that racket down the hall? That's the division general manager's monthly staff meeting. It's a real roar this time. Let's look in on it.

Paul Swampson, the division general manager, is "addressing" John Peoples, his manager of manufacturing: "John, for the third straight month you've badly missed your shipping schedules. We've missed our sales billed budgets something awful, and I'm getting terrible heat from Corporate up in Chicago. They won't stand for it. When are you going to get your act organized? I can't take much more of this nonsense."

John swallows, answers, "Yeah, I know we're badly behind our schedules — I've slapped on a lot of overtime these past weeks — but it's not really all our fault. You know, for the past four or five months the product drawings and material bills have been late from engineering, and those engineering change notices are killing us. Here, look at this study my materials manager made of problems with engineering documents coming to us late. See over here in the first column. . . ."

Swampson let's him have it — both barrels, full bore, between the eyes: "John, don't you ever again try to foist the blame off on someone else. Missed shipments are *manufacturing* problems. You're the manager of manufacturing. You solve 'em. If you can't . . . well, we'll see. We're talking about manufacturing problems now, not about engineering. We'll get to engineering later."

And he does. After about a half hour, Swampson pauses, pulls back the hammer, and let's fly a shot at Bob Atcheson, the manager of product engineering. "Bob, what's this about late engineering information to manufacturing — can't you guys in engineering keep up with your job? And how about all those engineering change notices — I keep hearing about them — can't you do your job right in the first place? Why keep changing?"

Bob's ready. "Well, Paul, we've fallen behind a little, and my group has also thrown on some overtime. But you know the real problem is that field sales is selling more and more of those special, nonstandard valves, and every order needs about twice as long to design, and the customers keep changing their specifications, so. . . ."

Bam! The general manager let's fly again: "Bob, I get so sick and tired of the way you guys point the blame at each other all the time. Why don't you solve your own problems, and let the other department managers solve theirs. Whenever we start to look at a problem in one department, you always point the finger to another department. I don't know why you are not good enough managers to take the blame when you're wrong instead of trying to pass the buck. . . ."

Well, come on. Let's get out of there. All of us who have been around for a while have heard that sort of discussion dozens of times. We don't have to hear it again. But it does lead us to the last rule for productivity improvement in the professional, knowledge, office sector:

Rule 4: What appears to be a major problem in an organization, often is only a symptom of an even greater problem in another organization.

Organizational theorists as well as practical business managers agree that we can improve delegation and management of responsibilities if we divide businesses into departments. This is fine for day-by-day management direction.

However, major productivity improvement requires an interdepartmental viewpoint. Figure 7.1 illustrates this and shows the main-line processes for a typical equipment manufacturing business. Commercial orders are the principal external demand that starts the process, which is completed when products and services are shipped to the customers, and operating results are summarized.

This is a highly simplified flow. In fact, the actual process is shaped more like a Christmas tree. A few external demands start the process at the top, and before it is over, dozens of demands and functions have spread throughout the business.

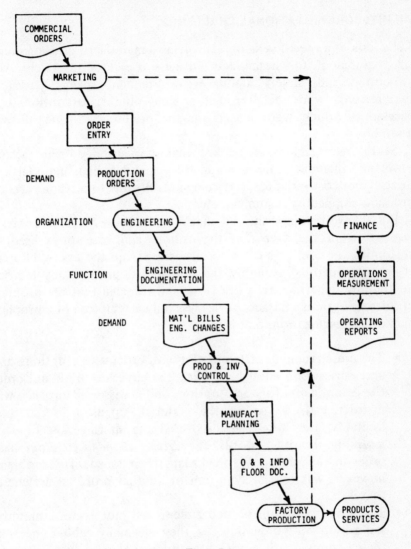

Figure 7.1

Here is an important point. As Rule 4 suggests, the actions of the upstream organizations greatly influence the characteristics of the demands they place on downstream groups. Therefore, the actions in one organization greatly influence the productivity of the other groups in the business.

AN INTERORGANIZATIONAL CHALLENGE

Let's look at a specific example involving a manufacturer of medium-size equipment for home and business use. Products were well structured and largely standardized. Frequent special customer requirements were met through a large number of options and accessories which were placed on the products at time of final assembly.

Senior management recognized that they suffered from factory problems, including missed shipment schedules, high material and direct labor cost variances, service complaints due to missing parts on products shipped to customers, etc.

Initial investigations showed that most of these factory problems resulted from the fact that the options and accessories used to customize the products often were missing from the assembly areas at the time of final assembly and shipment. Further study focused on the interdepartmental work flow, and revealed that the problem of missing options and accessories was only a symptom of a problem in another organization, that is:

- The purchasing department did not order these options and accessories soon enough. In fact, the buyer often did not order the components for these options and accessories until she was instructed to do so by the material expeditor in the final assembly area when he discovered the shortages at time of assembly. In other words, the *driving demand,* the purchase order to the vendor, was weeks late when issued. This problem, however, was only a symptom of another problem elsewhere, that is:

- The inventory control department did not issue a material requisition to purchasing, as they normally would, because these components were not monitored and requisitioned through the regular inventory control system. That is, the *driving demand,* the regular material requisition, was never issued. However, this problem was only a symptom of another problem elsewhere, that is:

- The design engineering department did not list the components for these options and accessories on the regular product bill of material. In other words, the driving demand for the inventory control system — the product bill of material — was incomplete, inadequate. Nevertheless, this problem, serious though it was, was only a symptom of a problem in another department, that is: The product marketing department had never clearly defined the product line to include these options and accessories as standard items, available for regular sale to customers, which in practice they were. Actually, the product manager responsible for these products recognized that these options and accessories were often ordered, but assumed that "someone down the line would handle the paperwork" to get them on the individual customer orders.

In summary, what appeared to be a problem in the factory assembly area was, in fact, only a symptom of a problem in purchasing, which was a symptom of a problem in inventory control, which was a symptom of a problem in design engineering, which was a symptom of the *real* problem in product marketing.

Once this real problem was identified, the product manager solved it by introducing these options and accessories as standard items in the regular product line — and then the "factory assembly" problem was solved.

SUMMARY

Studies show that 50–80% of all potential productivity improvement involves work flow *between* departments in a business.

In contrast, many older work simplification efforts concentrated on work flow *within* a single department, often within a small part of that department. Even today, we see experts in order entry, engineering documentation, word processing, inventory control, etc. Important though these specialized efforts are, they frequently miss the biggest potential improvements — interorganizational improvements.

Managers who seek real productivity improvement in the professional, knowledge, office activities of their business should concentrate on this interorganizational work flow.

Part II
The Method of Operation
Function Analysis

Chapter 8
Senior Management
Introduction and Planning

The second part of this book, Chapters 8–13, describes the O.F.A. method, the step-by-step process to improve the productivity of your organization. Not only will you learn how to use O.F.A. as an integrated approach, but you can lift out of O.F.A. many of the techniques described here, and use them with whatever other improvement methods you may be using now.

Experience with companies that have used O.F.A. shows that it works best to divide the program into three separate yet related phases:

Phase 1. Senior management introduction and planning
Phase 2. Middle management analysis and recommendation
Phase 3. Improvement implementation.

The responsibility for each phase is clearly assigned, and each phase is completed before moving on to the next, as illustrated in Figure 8.1.

Through their Phase 1, the senior managers establish and demonstrate their commitment, and develop the objectives, scope, participation and schedule for the remainder of the O.F.A. program.

During Phase 2, the middle management O.F.A. team analyzes the activities within the assigned scope, identifies potential improvements, and recommends specific changes to achieve these improvements. The O.F.A. team then reports the recommended improvements back to the senior managers, who review, modify and accept them.

In Phase 3, the O.F.A. team members, along with their colleagues, implement the accepted recommendations, under the direction of the senior managers.

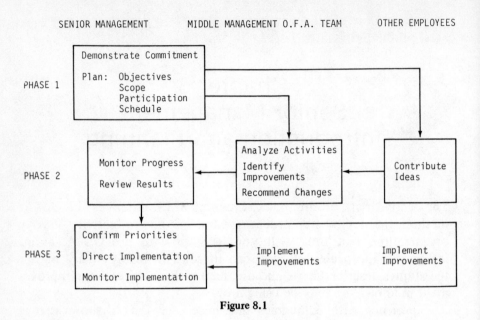

Figure 8.1

With this brief overview, let's now focus on Phase 1. As suggested before, this first phase has three objectives:

1. To establish a senior management commitment to productivity improvement through Operation Function Analysis
2. To train senior managers in O.F.A. to the extent they can carry out their responsibilities in the program
3. To develop an initial plan for the remainder of the O.F.A. program.

SENIOR MANAGEMENT COMMITMENT

The oldest cliché in business is this: Senior management commitment is essential to the success of a program. Too often this consists of a one-hour perfunctory meeting at the start of the program, during which senior managers confirm they are "100% behind the program," and "give it their full support."

This simply is not adequate for something as important as productivity improvement. Mr. Paul Elsen, Director of Executive Development for Honeywell, Inc., stated in reference to his company's general productivity activities:

A company productivity improvement program starts with commitment from the senior executives. They must be dedicated to the premise that a viable, visible, disciplined, and organized approach to productivity improvement throughout the organization is desirable and necessary for attaining the key operating goals, such as profit, return on assets, service level, and growth. Without it, a company program at best can be no more than a collection of partial programs often counterproductive to each other.

Mr. Elsen pointed out that there must be more than just a commitment to the general concept of productivity improvement. He continued:

There must be a genuine willingness to challenge traditions and what the internal culture of the organization has defined as acceptable behavior.
But even this level of commitment is not enough. Productivity improvement is not a spectator sport. Senior managers must demonstrate this commitment to improvement through real involvement and leadership. They must initiate the productivity improvement program, must lead it through its course, and assume responsibility for its success.

SENIOR MANAGEMENT TRAINING

Every Phase 1 program begins with a one-day intensive training seminar for the senior managers. In a typical small to medium-size company, this would include the president and his vice presidents of sales, manufacturing, finance, engineering, human resources, etc. In a division of a larger company, it would include the division general manager, and his similar subordinate managers. In a medium-size, non-teaching hospital, it might include at a minimum the administrator and his assistant administrators of patient services, nursing services, general services, finance, and personnel and training, with appropriate representation from the medical staff and residency programs. In short, the senior managers are the half dozen or so people who have the senior operating responsibility for the day-by-day work of the organization.

I often meet people who say, "Impossible. I can't even get the senior managers to sit still for anything longer than an hour! Anyway, all this training is just a bunch of window dressing. It's really not necessary — just a waste of time for all of us."

Wrong. Never underestimate the need and the benefit of thorough training, in an O.F.A. program or any other similar effort. Mr. Edward L. Maier, Vice President of Xerox, speaking about his company's general productivity programs, had this to say about training:

Time spent on training and familiarization, although sometimes considered unproductive and costly, if carried out carefully, pays dividends later.

The immediate goal of the Phase 1 seminar should be to train the senior managers to the point where *they* can decide for *themselves* how to best use O.F.A., or any method, to improve the productivity of *their* organization. Remember the emphasis on do-it-yourself in Chapter 2? Well, it begins right here, with the senior managers.

The one-day seminar should present information on the O.F.A. logic, method, and use. It should be light on elegant theory, and heavy on practical application. Table 8.1 shows a time distribution that works well.

Table 8.1. Senior Management Seminar.

SUBJECT	PERCENT OF SEMINAR
Description of O.F.A. logic, as presented in Chapters 1–6	25
Description of O.F.A. method (Chapters 7–13)	25
Presentation of case studies that illustrate O.F.A. logic and method	50

SENIOR MANAGEMENT PLANNING

After the senior managers have completed their one-day training seminar, they should devote at least another eight hours to individual and group working sessions during which they develop a plan for the remainder of their O.F.A. program. This plan typically focuses on five factors:

1. *Program objectives:* the benefits that senior management wants to get from the total O.F.A. program
2. *Program scope:* the areas of the total organization that should be included in the program
3. *Program participation:* the people who will conduct the subsequent Phase 2 (middle management analysis and recommendation)
4. *Program scheduling:* the timing of the Phase 2 start, end, and level of effort required from the participants
5. *Program communications:* the specific steps that will be taken to inform all employees about the O.F.A. program.

O.F.A. Program Objectives

Senior managers should establish objectives and goals for their O.F.A. program which require demonstrable productivity improvements, are measurable wherever possible, and can be used for evaluation of the O.F.A. program and those involved in it. Here are some guidelines that will help you do this.

Concentrate Your Fire

As you establish your goals, select a limited number of target areas which you believe have the greatest need and potential for improvement, and focus your O.F.A. program on these. Every organization has a maximum rate of change, a maximum number of innovations that can be introduced at one time. Recognize and do not exceed yours. Do not diffuse your productivity efforts.

Set General Objectives

Within each target area, the senior managers should define their objectives in broad terms. If the objectives set in Phase 1 are too narrow, they can constrain the thinking of the middle managers in the subsequent Phase 2, which in turn can result in unimaginative, even trivial improvement recommendations.

Here is an example of a narrow goal: "Reduce inventory level." There is only one reasonable response. Reduce inventory regardless of the consequences.

Here is an example of a broader goal: "Improve inventory management." This can encourage many responses, such as improving inventory turnover, raising customer service levels, reducing production cycle time, increasing factory productivity, etc.

Go for the Long Haul

Emphasize strategy over tactics. Be prepared to accept minor, short-range setbacks to achieve long-term benefits. Senior managers should build this long-haul perspective into their O.F.A. program plan. Otherwise, people will by nature focus on immediate, even cosmetic changes.

Establish Audacious Goals

Senior managers should not be afraid to establish very ambitious objectives for their O.F.A. program. Never underestimate the knowledge and cleverness of the people who do the day-by-day work in an organization. It is much better to set a very broad, demanding objective, and fall short of it, than to set a very modest objective, and easily achieve it.

Plan for Quality

Some people believe there is a conflict between productivity and quality of products and services. Indeed, as recently as 1980, the annual report of a leading company stated, "Emphasis on productivity will not be made at the expense of quality."

This is fuzzy thinking. There can be no conflict between quality and productivity in a successful company. In fact, each is an integral element of the other. Quality leads to productivity, and productivity to quality. *Example:* The Japanese automobile industry has grown from essentially nothing to a major force on the combination of quality and productivity. *Example:* The Black and Decker Company leads its market on the basis of these same two factors. Senior managers must be sure that their O.F.A. program plan recognizes this compatibility and interdependence.

Seek People Improvement

It is not enough just to aim for work flow improvement. Your O.F.A. program also should improve the people who perform this work flow, their skills and knowledge of the business. Chapter 2 describes the benefits that can be gained by this emphasis. Some of this will occur in any case, but it will be much more effective if the stated objectives of your O.F.A. program specifically include people improvement.

At the beginning of this section, we stated that Phase 1 senior management planning should focus on five aspects of the O.F.A. program: objectives, scope, participation, scheduling and communications. You have just read about the first. Now let's move on to the second, program scope — that is, the activities of your organization that should be included in your O.F.A. program.

O.F.A. Program Scope

The scope of your O.F.A. program should be as broad as practicable. But what does this mean? How do you define scope? How do you know when you have enough scope? If the scope is too broad, you will diffuse your efforts and accomplish little. If too narrow, many potential improvements will be missed.

The scope of your O.F.A. program should be defined in terms of two factors: functions and organizations. Let's examine each of these individually, and then see how you can combine them to establish a satisfactory scope for your program.

Scope in Terms of Functions

In Chapter 6 you read that functions are the basic building blocks of work flow, and that the activities of your organization can be viewed as a network of these functions and the demands that drive them. Look again at the lists of functions for a typical equipment manufacturing business and for a hospital. Notice how in each case the functions can be collected into broad categories.

The first step in defining the scope of your O.F.A. program is to decide which major categories of functions will be included in your program, and which will be omitted. For example, the senior managers of a major operating division in an equipment manufacturing company might reasonably decide to include all three major categories of functions as shown in Chapter 6. On the other hand, the senior managers of a subsidiary manufacturing plant might reasonably decide to omit the entire first category, the preliminary processes, because very little of their time is devoted to these activities, and they wish to focus their O.F.A. program on the main-line and supporting processes.

After this first review of the main categories, go back through them and identify any major functions within each category that you should handle as an exception. For example, the senior managers in the operating division might examine the first category — the preliminary processes — and decide to include only certain functions:

- Product planning and development
- Resource planning and development
- Manufacturing standards development
- Manufacturing facilities development.

The remaining functions in the preliminary processes would be omitted because they were not significant nor of major concern at this time.

Similarly, these same senior managers might decide to include within the scope of their O.F.A. program all the functions associated with acquiring and stocking material for manufacturing *except* those concerned with the purchasing activities. They would omit those because they are performed largely by a central, corporate purchasing organization not within their division.

Caution. At this early stage of your O.F.A. program, the work flow functions will not be clearly defined. In fact, this will not occur until well into the subsequent Phase 2. Senior managers should not let this uncertainty handicap them. Prepare a "first pass" list of functions based on your judgment and knowledge of your business. It will be satisfactory for your Phase 1 planning.

Scope in Terms of Organizations

The next step in defining the scope of your program is to review the departments and sections within your total organization and identify those which you want to include and those to omit, regardless of the functions they perform.

For example, the senior managers of the operating division in the manufacturing business might decide to include all organizations located at their main facility, but to omit the field sales and warehousing departments scattered around the country. They would *exclude* these departments — to facilitate the conduct of the O.F.A. program — even though the people in them may perform some of the functions already *included* within the scope of the O.F.A. program.

Combined Scope

Once you have defined the scope both in terms of functions and organizations, list them on a matrix as shown in Figure 8.2, with the functions down the left, and the organizations across the top. Obviously, the figure is only a small portion of the total matrix for a real business. such a total matrix would cover several pages, and include perhaps 100 functions and 15 organizations.

Select the first function, for example, sales liaison. Move across the matrix and place a check mark under every organization that in your senior management judgment devotes a significant amount of time to that function. Then ask yourself:

1. Do we feel that most of the effort devoted to that function comes from the organizations checked on the matrix?
2. Is there another organization, not yet listed on the matrix, that devotes a significant time to that function?
3. Should we add that organization to our matrix?
4. If only a few organizations work on that function, perhaps the function is not significant to our analysis. Should we drop it from our matrix?

Functions \ Organizations	Field Sales	Internal Sales	Product Eng'g.	Materials Mngt.	Factory Supervision	Service Parts	Accounting
Sales liaison	√	√					
Direct selling	√						
Application eng'g.	√		√				
Cost estimating			√				√
Proposal preparation		√	√			√	
Order editing		√	√			√	
Order entry		√				√	
Order acknowledgment		√				√	
Order follow-up		√		√	√	√	
Order control		√		√	√		
Order monitoring		√		√	√		

Figure 8.2

After you have reviewed the functions, look back at the organizations shown across the head of the matrix, pick the first, and ask:

1. Does this first organization contribute significantly to one or more functions, or only lightly to the functions listed?
2. If it contributes only lightly, should we remove the organization from the matrix and the scope of the program?
3. On the other hand, does this organization devote a large proportion of its effort to a function not listed on the matrix?
4. Should this function be added to the matrix and the scope of the program?

Working in this manner, the senior managers will be able to defined the scope of their O.F.A. program so as to include the principal functions as well as departments and sections involved in the activities of their total organization.

O.F.A. Program Participation

After the senior managers have planned the objectives and scope of their program, as described in the preceding sections, they then should plan the program participation, that is, select the members of the O.F.A. team who will conduct the subsequent Phase 2. The success of the program will quite literally depend on the quality of the O.F.A. team, so this selection should be done carefully and well.

Caution. Notice the word *select.* Volunteers are not accepted nor are nominations solicited from subordinate managers. The senior managers themselves, after adequate O.F.A. training, should select the members of the O.F.A. team, based on certain criteria outlined here.

Include Organizations Throughout the Scope

As far as possible, the O.F.A. team should include at least one person from each organization within the program scope. There are three reasons for this. First, it ensures that the O.F.A. team will have a basic familiarity with all areas within the scope, and this will facilitate the collection and analysis of the information, as described in Chapters 9 and 10. Second, it provides an informal contact between the O.F.A. program and all areas of the organization. Third, no group will feel left out, and this will enhance the eventual implementation of the final recommended improvements.

Caution. Although the team members are drawn from many groups, they do not *represent* these groups in a legislative sense. That is, each member does not look out for the interest of his own department. There are no votes in the Phase 2 process where one person casts the engineering vote, another the manufacturing vote, and a third the marketing vote. They are all members of the O.F.A. *team* first, and representatives of their organizations second.

Deemphasize Rank

All O.F.A. team members need not be at the same middle management level. Rank is unimportant. All that counts inside the O.F.A. team work room is knowledge and a creative attitude.

A typical O.F.A. team might include managers, supervisors and various specialists. For instance, one very successful O.F.A. team in a medium-size division of a large manufacturing company included the following people:

Division controller
Supervisor of quality control
Product marketing specialist
Manager of materials
Order documentation specialist
Manager of personnel
Supervisor of production control
Chief industrial engineer
Senior product design engineer
General foreman of final assembly
Supervisor of engineering documentation
Manager of purchasing
Supervisor of service parts department
Internal sales and order entry specialist
Chief product design engineer

Balance Experience with Freshness

Your O.F.A. team should include several people with deep experience in your organization. Even though they may have seldom expressed them, they will have hundreds of ideas as a result of their experience and knowledge. Balance this with several people who are quite new in your organization and can bring fresh ideas.

For example, one successful O.F.A. team included a member who was within six months of retirement and a recent Harvard M.B.A. Another O.F.A. team included a manufacturing general foreman, a real "bull of the woods" with over 30 years factory experience, and a young accounting supervisor with two years experience in the division.

Once you establish the extremes of old line conservatism and audacious freshness, then fill the middle with "regulars," and you will have a good O.F.A. team.

You will gain two benefits from such a mixture of members. First, the team members will gain a broad understanding of the business and of their coworkers. This will improve their ability to work within the organization long after the end of the formal O.F.A. program. Second, it will help ensure that the final recommended improvements are balanced, factoring in both the experience of the past and the freshness of the future.

Seek Constructive Attitudes

Despite all that has been said before, a team member's attitude is more important than his organizational base, his position level, or his experience. He must have a constructive attitude, a genuine desire to work with others to improve the productivity of his business through all available methods, including O.F.A.

Select Respect

Senior managers should select O.F.A. team members who have the broad respect of others based on their knowledge, experience, training, innovative attitudes, and natural leadership.

There are three reasons why this respect is needed. First, it enables team members to work together effectively. Second, it ensures acceptance by their colleagues outside the team as they conduct their Phase 2 program. Third, with the respect of others, the final recommendations will be more easily accepted and implemented.

Develop Human Resources

Every person involved in a productivity improvement program such as O.F.A. will gain new knowledge and skills, increased exposure to his peers and senior managers, and will be able to contribute more effectively to his organization.

Senior managers should exploit this opportunity by assigning to the O.F.A. team those who will benefit from this development, and will return these benefits to the business.

Balance the Load

In the preceding paragraphs, we have described characteristics you should seek in the individual O.F.A. team members. But the question remains, how many people should serve on the team to ensure a balanced work load? The size of the O.F.A. team is determined by the size of the organization, and the scope of the total O.F.A. program. Here is an easy rule-of-thumb way to estimate the size of the O.F.A. team for a typical, medium-size business:

1. Determine the size of the population, that is, the number of people involved in the activities within the scope of the program.
2. Divide the population size by 4 to determine the number of interviews the O.F.A. team will conduct during their Phase 2 information collection process.
3. Divide the number of interviews by 7 to get the number of members on the O.F.A. team.

For example, a medium-size manufacturing business has a population of 380 people involved within the program scope. It will need about 95 interviews (380/4 = 95), and about fourteen O.F.A. team members (95/7 = 13.6). Figure 8.3 shows data for three typical companies, and can serve as a further guide. For larger organizations,

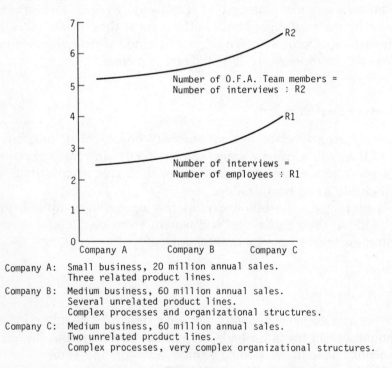

Company A: Small business, 20 million annual sales.
            Three related product lines.
Company B: Medium business, 60 million annual sales.
            Several unrelated product lines.
            Complex processes and organizational structures.
Company C: Medium business, 60 million annual sales.
            Two unrelated prcduct lines.
            Complex processes, very complex organizational structures.

Figure 8.3

with groups of people doing more or less the same type of work, these divisors become significantly larger, and the number of interviews and the size of the O.F.A. team become proportionately smaller. Final selection must be based on experience and judgment.

The O.F.A. Team Leader

The last step for senior managers as they plan program participation is to designate one of the Phase 2 team members as the team leader. As the name suggests, this person will be the administrative ramrod. He will coordinate the work of the team, and serve as principal liaison between the team and the senior managers.

We have found no preferred background for the team leader. Successful leaders have included a manager of sales engineering, a supervisor of service parts inventory control, a manufacturing general superintendant, a division controller, a manager of computer systems. Each was a natural leader, well respected by all others in the organization, with a bent for project management.

O.F.A. Program Schedule

The fourth element of the O.F.A. program plan is the Phase 2 schedule. Productivity improvement must be a conscious, continuing part of every person's job. Time must be allocated for this work, and the first step is the definition of the Phase 2 schedule by the senior managers.

At this point, they should be concerned with only two dates, the Phase 2 start and finish. Schedule details will be refined by the O.F.A. Team during the first week of their Phase 2.

Phase 2 Start Date

If possible, at least a month should elapse between Phase 1 and the beginning of Phase 2, to allow time for two things. First, each O.F.A. team member and his immediate manager should reschedule and/or reassign some of the team member's work to allow him to participate in the program and also continue with his regular assignments.

The second reason for this break is even more important. It allows time for the senior managers to inform all employees about the O.F.A.

program plan, the first step in a line of communications that will continue throughout the program.

Phase 2 Completion Date

Using the ratios shown in Figure 8.3, a typical, medium-size Phase 2 program will require 11–14 weeks to complete. The elapsed time will depend on the level of effort applied by the O.F.A. team. Most of O.F.A. team members devote about 30% of their time to Phase 2.

A larger team, and/or a heavier than 30% application rate will shorten this time, but it will be much harder to coordinate the effort. A smaller team, and/or lighter than 30% application will lengthen the elapse time for Phase 2, with a great danger that the program will drag, and interest will wain.

Caution. Senior managers should set a firm completion date for Phase 2. In a field as fertile as productivity improvement, the team can continue forever, gathering fine ideas and potential improvements. It is much better to set a firm completion date and take what you have on that date. Refinements can come later during the Phase 3 (improvement implementation).

Program Communications

In a participative, do-it-yourself program such as O.F.A., there should be no secrets. Be open and up-front. Keep all employees completely informed.

In a typical O.F.A. program, this communication goes far beyond the usual letters and bulletin board statements. At a minimum it should consist of meetings with all employees within the scope of the program. Senior managers would use these meetings to:

- Describe the productivity needs of the business
- Outline the steps leading up to the use of O.F.A.
- Briefly describe the O.F.A. process, including the heavy involvement by many employees
- Request their continuing support for the program.

SUMMARY

An Operation Function Analysis program begins with senior management introduction and planning, which involves three factors:

First, senior managers must demonstrate a total commitment to productivity improvement. They must exhibit a real willingness to challenge traditional practices, and lead others to do the same.

Next, senior managers must train for their role in the program, so that they can decide for themselves how O.F.A. can best be used to improve the productivity of their organization.

Finally, senior managers must develop a preliminary plan for Phase 2 (middle management analysis and recommendation). The execution of this plan and the conduct of Phase 2 are described in the Chapters 9–12.

Chapter 9
Information Collection

The preceding chapter described the first phase of your O.F.A. program, senior management introduction and planning, during which the senior managers establish the program objectives, scope, participation and general schedules.

The O.F.A. program now moves on to the second phase, middle management analysis and recommendation. This will be conducted by the O.F.A. team, a group of middle managers, supervisors and senior specialists selected by the senior managers from organizations within the program scope. The Team members will analyze the organization's activities and work flow, identify potential improvements and the changes needed to achieve these improvements, and plan the implementation of these changes.

This will be accomplished through the four steps that comprise Phase 2:

1. Information collection (this chapter)
2. Information analysis (Chapter 10)
3. Evaluation and improvement identification (Chapter 11)
4. Recommendation and implementation planning (Chapter 12).

Before starting these four steps, the O.F.A. team members must do two things. First, they must be trained in the O.F.A. method. Second, they must plan in detail all four steps of their Phase 2.

THE O.F.A. TEAM – TRAINING AND PLANNING

O.F.A. Team Training

In a typical O.F.A. program, the team members devote about 20–30 hours to formal training in the use of O.F.A., based on the material in this book. Training can be conducted by anyone skilled in O.F.A., a team leader from an earlier O.F.A. program, the corporate productivity manager with special training in O.F.A., or an external consultant experienced in O.F.A.

No matter what participative improvement method you use, O.F.A., Quality Circles, or something else, do not slight this initial training. Good training is absolutely vital to the success of any participative improvement program. Don't neglect it.

O.F.A. Team Planning

After they have completed their training, the O.F.A. team members plan their Phase 2 program. In essence, they refine the plans that their senior managers developed during the earlier Phase 1 planning sessions. In a typical O.F.A. program, the team devotes about 8 hours to this planning, following the process described here.

Refine Objectives and Scope

Because team members have a more detailed understanding of the work processes, they often can identify specific objectives overlooked by the senior managers, and can extend or contract the program scope to correspond with these refined objectives. Later, they will review these modifications with the senior managers, and agree on a final set of objectives and scope.

Caution. Do not be surprised if you change some of the objectives and scope as the program progresses through Phase 2. You'll get smarter as you go, and should be able to continually improve the objectives and scope, often up to the very end of Phase 2. Remember, however, hold firm to the scheduled completion date.

Identify Principal Functions

After the team members have confirmed the program objectives and scope, they next identify the principal functions performed within the program scope. At this point, go back to Chapter 6 and familiarize yourself again with the concept of functions. Remember, the functions listed there are for a typical organization. Your functions may be similar, or totally different.

Next, check with the senior managers and get the list of functions they prepared when they originally defined the program scope in Phase 1, and the function/organization matrix illustrated in Figure 8.2.

Working as a team, refine that list and matrix. Again, don't try to be perfect, but be sure that the function list and matrix match the refined project objectives and scope. At this point, some O.F.A. users identify the major demands that drive these functions, and draw a preliminary flow diagram based on these demands and functions. Such an initial review of the work flow will help you more effectively plan the information collection process, as described in the following sections.

Identify Sources of Information

The team members now identify the sources from which they will collect the information they will use during their Phase 2. The principal source will be interviews with people who actually perform the work within the scope.

Perhaps the easiest way to identify the people you need to interview is to use the function/organization matrix, after you have refined it, as illustrated in Figure 9.1. Remember, this is only a portion of the total matrix for a real business.

Focus on the first organization, e.g., field sales. Scan down that column, and identify and list the person who is most knowledgeable in each function performed within that organization. Place a number in that matrix cell to represent that person. Notice that a given person may easily be involved in more than one cell.

Remember. You are seeking knowledge. Do not limit your interviews to supervisors, lead workers, senior "experts," etc. Instead get down and interview the people who carry out the day-by-day work. Find out what *really* happens, not what is *supposed* to happen.

After this, move to the next organization, e.g., internal sales, and repeat the process, on across through the whole set of organizations and functions. When finished, you will have your list of interviewees, which for our very simplified case might appear as in Table 9.1.

Finally, hold the interview list out at arm's length and see if it makes sense. Are there functions or organizations still missing, or

Functions / Organizations	Field Sales	Internal Sales	Product Eng'g.	Materials Mngnt.	Factory Supervision	Service Parts	Accounting
Sales liaison	1 √	3 √					
Direct selling	1 √						
Application eng'g.	2 √		6 √				
Cost estimating			7 √				13 √
Proposal preparation		3 √	6 √			10 √	
Order editing		4 √	6 √			11 √	
Order entry		4 √				11 √	
Order acknowledgment		4 √				11 √	
Order follow-up		5 √		8 √	9 √	12 √	
Order control		5 √		8 √	9 √		
Order monitoring		5 √		8 √	9 √		

Figure 9.1

extraneous? Can you consolidate and reduce the number of interviews? Is the person listed really the best source of information on these activities?

Through this process, you will be able to identify at least 90% of the interviews you will need for your information collection, and the others will become obvious as Phase 2 progresses. Do not worry about getting a "scientific sample." Just interview enough people to get a good understanding of the activities under study. Use your judgment. No fixed rules exist.

In addition to the interviews, the team will identify other sources of information, such as reports from previous studies, regular operating reports, etc. Make a list of these other information sources, too.

Plan and Organize the Interviews

Once you have identified the interviewees, then group them into logical interviewing modules, where each module includes a set of related activities.

For example, in our illustration, we might have the following groups of interviews:

Table 9.1. List of Interviewees.

NO.	INTERVIEWEE	ORGANIZATION	FUNCTION
1	George Andrews	Field sales	Sales liaison Direct selling
2	Pete Labowski	Field sales	Application eng'g.
3	Jason Forrester	Internal sales	Sales liaison Proposal preparation
4	Bill Speaker	Internal sales	Order editing Order entry Order acknowledgment
5	Margaret Choy	Internal sales	Order follow-up Order control Order monitoring
6	Clayton Zink	Product eng'g.	Application eng'g. Proposal preparation Order editing
7	Randy Johnson	Product eng'g.	Cost estimating
8	Rob Forbush	Mat'ls mgt.	Order follow-up Order control Order monitoring
9	Jeff Lamesa	Factory superv.	Order follow-up Order control Order monitoring
10	Andy Banks	Service parts	Proposal preparation
11	Walker Bowzer	Service parts	Order editing Order entry Order acknowledgment
12	Lauren Larue	Service parts	Order follow-up
13	Jake Petloff	Accounting	Cost estimating

Module 1: All activities in field sales and internal sales which precede the receipt of the order (Interviews 1, 2 and 3)

Module 2: All activities in internal sales related to getting the order into the backlog (4)

Module 3: All activities in internal sales related to following, monitoring, and controlling an order as it is processed through the business (5)

Module 4: All activities in product engineering which precede the receipt of the order, and also related to getting the order into the backlog (6 and 7)

Module 5: All activities in materials management and factory supervision related to following, monitoring, and controlling
an order through the business (8 and 9)

Module 6: All activities in the service parts organization (10, 11,
and 12)

Module 7: All activities in the accounting organization (13).

Two important points:

1. This is only one arrangement of modules or groups. Some
other arrangement might be just as logical, or even more
so. For example, perhaps we should group all activities
concerned with work preceding the receipt of the order,
that is, interviews, 1, 2, 3, 6, 7, 10, and 13. Similarly,
perhaps we should group all work associated with following,
monitoring, and controlling the order, that is, interviews 5, 8,
9, and 12.

2. In a real situation, you will have many more modules, each
containing several interviews. Once you have identified the
interviewing modules, then divide the entire O.F.A. team into
two-person interviewing teams, and assign one or more
modules to each team. Ideally, one person should be familiar
with the activities within that group of interviews. The other
person should be from a part of the organization that precedes
or follows these activities. Don't worry if you do not have a
perfect match between each two-person team and its interview
modules. As the information collection progresses, you will
see that certain interviewing teams are more heavily loaded
than others, and reassignments can be made when this occurs.

Single Versus Multiple Interviews. Although nearly all interviews
will involve a single interviewee, in a few cases you may wish to
interview two or more people at the same time. This is appropriate
when several people do essentially the same work, and more reliable
estimates can be obtained more efficiently by interviewing these
people together, and averaging the results as you go along.

Schedule Phase 2 in Detail

Let's recap where we are. The O.F.A. team members have been
trained, and are planning their Phase 2 program. They have refined

the objectives and scope, identified principal functions within the scope and the sources of information on these functions. Then they planned and organized the information collection interviews needed to gather this information. Now, to complete their planning, the team members will prepare a time schedule for Phase 2.

Based on the experience of a number of companies which have used O.F.A., the average percentages of time devoted to the four steps in Phase 2 are as follows:

Information collection	29%
Information analysis	14%
Evaluation and improvement identification	22%
Recommendation and implementation planning	35%

Experience shows that these proportions remain about the same for quite a range of program size, from small to large. Therefore, if you can estimate the time required for information collection, you can proportion the time required for the other three steps, and determine the overall time schedule.

Each interview will require about two hours to conduct, and another hour or so to review and clean up your notes and documentation. Early interviews may require more time, later ones less. Assume you have 95 interviews planned, with each consuming 3¼ hours to conduct and review, for a total of 309 hours of interviewing. With fourteen people on the O.F.A. team, you will have 7 interviewing teams, and on that basis you will devote 44 elapsed hours to the information collection step. From this you can estimate the following total time for Phase 2:

Information collection	29%	44 hours
Information analysis	14%	21 hours
Evaluation and improvement identification	22%	33 hours
Recommendation and implementation planning	35%	53 hours
	100%	151 hours

That is, Phase 2 will consume about 150 hours elapsed time. As a short cut, use this formula for estimating the time required for information collection:

$$\text{Elapsed time} = \frac{\text{No. of interviews} \times 40}{\text{No. people in team} \times R_2}$$

where R_2 is the factor shown in Figure 8.3, and used by the senior managers to determine the size of the O.F.A. team.

So, summarizing to this point, the O.F.A. team has been trained, and now has planned Phase 2. You are now ready to begin the first step in Phase 2, information collection.

INFORMATION COLLECTION – THE NEED

One often hears a manager or supervisor say, "Oh, we know all about the activities in our department. It's all in our procedures manual: flow charts, position descriptions, and everything. Besides, we already know what our problems are, and what kind of new systems we need. We don't need to waste time collecting more information."

Wrong. You seldom know as much about your own organization's activities as you think you do. Careful review and analysis frequently show that the work flow is much more complex, and has only the most general resemblance to the official procedures documented by the business.

Since productivity improvement requires solid knowledge of these activities, you should gather two types of information:

1. *Quantitative:* demand volumes, hours of effort, cycle times, external expenses, etc.
2. *Qualitative:* specific observations, suggestions, and recommendations by the people who do the day-by-day work.

Information collection may sound easy. Just go out, ask some questions, perhaps pass around a few survey sheets, note down the answers, and that's that. It is not that easy. It requires specific skills and attitudes, and the rest of this chapter is devoted to these.

THE INFORMATION COLLECTION INTERVIEW

There are many ways to collect information for productivity improvement. Some people prefer a time study, work measurement approach, where precise records are kept of time devoted to specific operations, frequency of events, etc. There is a place for this, especially in the clerical areas.

However, users of O.F.A. have found these traditional time study and work sampling methods are not really applicable to the nonrepetitive activities in knowledge work, and more valid results usually can be obtained by estimates gathered through interviews with the people who do the work.

In addition to more valid results, direct interviewing brings another benefit — broader participation. As a result of this interviewing, many other people in the organization get involved in the O.F.A. program. Hence, they too feel they have a role in and responsibility for productivity improvement in their part of the organization, and so they contribute their ideas to this improvement. For these reasons, the direct interview is the principal information collection method used in Operation Function Analysis.

Three Types Of Interviews

There are three types of information collection interviews: scoping, work flow, and interface.

Scoping Interview

This type of interview usually is conducted with the manager or supervisor of a department or section to obtain a general overview of the activities within that part of the total organization. It identifies the broad functions carried on within the department, who does what in general terms, and major areas for further review and improvement. Typical questions in this type of interview are:

1. What are the principal responsibilities in your department?
2. What are the main demands that hit your department?
3. What major activities are carried out by your people to meet these demands?
4. How many people, and what type of positions are in your department?
5. What is the general work flow carried out by your people? Who does what, in overall terms?

Information gathered through a scoping interview often is used to plan subsequent work flow interviews in that same department, as well as interfacing interviews in other areas. Usually less than 5% of all interviews are scoping.

Work Flow Interview

This is the basic information collection interview. The objectives are:

- To collect information on the detailed activities performed by one person, or a small group of persons doing essentially the same work
- To gather ideas on how to improve the performance of these activities.

Work flow interviews typically comprise about 85% of all interviews. They will be described in greater detail and illustrated later in this chapter.

Interface Interview

Often activities within the scope of an O.F.A. program interface with activities and organizations outside the scope. Team members must understand these interfaces in order to improve internal productivity of activities within the program scope. Interface interviews are conducted with people in these neighboring organizations to gather information to provide this understanding. Often interface interviews concentrate on getting key observations, as described later in this chapter. Many of the best recommendations originate with interface interviews. About 10% of all interviews will be of this type, although this figure can rise to 20% if the organization under review is imbedded within a large, integrated corporation.

Prepare for the Interviews

Successful interviewing is not an inborn skill. In essentially all cases, special training and experience is necessary. Plan carefully for this step, because the success of the whole O.F.A. program depends on it.

First, review the list of interviews made as you planned Phase 2, as described earlier in this chapter. Make sure the interviews cover the program scope as completely as possible at this point. Watch out for the scoping and interface interviews. Although relatively few in number, they are important. Too often they are neglected until far into the information collection process, and do not receive adequate attention. Finally, confirm that each two-person team understands which interviews it will conduct.

Inform the Interviewees

Once you have established your interview plan and assigned responsibility for the interviews, then inform your interviewees. Since your interview schedule probably will not be completely firm, you may be able to inform only the first group of interviewees, and then inform the rest as your interviews progress and the schedule is firmed up.

A letter should be sent to all interviewees in which you:

- Make reference to the initial announcement of the O.F.A. program by the president or general manager
- Very briefly describe the O.F.A. approach and the need to gather information on current activities
- Indicate that the recipient has been selected for an interview
- State that no special preparation is needed, although it would be good if he would gather examples of principal documents and reports he receives or issues
- Inform him that a member of the O.F.A. team will contact him concerning time and place of the interview
- Stress that he should feel totally free to discuss any aspect of the O.F.A. program with any member of the O.F.A. team all of whose names are shown on this same letter.

This letter usually is signed by the O.F.A. team leader, with copies to the interviewee's immediate manager or supervisor.

Test the Interview Process

Because good interviewing is the key to a successful program, the O.F.A. team members should test their interviewing skills before continuing. Two people from the team should interview a third team member. The rest of the team should observe and note all ideas they have for improving the effectiveness of the interview. In most cases, two or three such role-play interviews are needed before the team members feel comfortable with the process.

The team then selects one of the regularly scheduled interviewees, and the responsible two-person team interviews this individual in the presence of all the other members. This requires an understanding and unflappable interviewee, and he should, of course, be told what is happening, that is, he is serving as the "final examination" in interviewing skills for the team members. When this is completed, you are ready to start interviewing.

Remember, do not slight the training and testing of the interview process. Success depends on it.

Interviewing — Step By Step

In this section, we will describe the principal steps in a typical work flow interview, and will illustrate these in a later section.

A Form of Conversation

The O.F.A. interview is a structured yet low-key way of gathering information on the activities of an organization. But there's a lot more to it than just asking a string of questions. Successful interviewing is a form of guided conversation, and is most successful when we use a wide range of conversational modes or responses.

Dr. Gerald Goodman, UCLA psychologist and expert on how people talk to each other, has identified six basic conversational responses which we can use to gather information in our O.F.A. interviews. They are: question, advisement, reflection, interpretation, self-disclosure, and silence.

One type of response is not necessarily better than another. Indeed, combine and mix your responses for a more interesting and effective interview. If we restrict ourselves to one or two types of responses, we limit the effectiveness of our interviews.

Let's illustrate these six responses by imagining that as part of an O.F.A. program at a large hospital complex, we are interviewing Jack Decker, manager of maintenance and repair services. Jack has just said to us, "I have to schedule hundreds of maintenance and repair requests each month. They aren't all the same, either. They fall into at least ten different types, or categories."

Question. "What are these different categories?"

This is a direct approach to gathering more information, and works perfectly well. Watch out, though, that you don't shoot off question after question, until you sound like a trial lawyer closing in on the accused. Avoid questions that can be answered with "yes" or "no." Seek broader, more informative answers.

Advisement. "We ought to identify each type of maintenance and repair request and write them down so we can talk about them further."

Advisement often is a direct statement to guide the interviewee, but it also can be an explanation of the interviewing process, the form sheets you are going to use, or the overall objectives of the O.F.A. program, etc. An advisement is a good way to start the O.F.A. interview, to break the ice, and to demonstrate that the interview does have some structure and organization.

Reflection. "That's interesting. I can understand how there could be a number of different types of maintenance problems in an hospital complex as large as this."

A reflection is just that. You reflect the statement, in a different form, back to the interviewee, to show that you have heard and understand what he has said. It reassures him, and shows understanding and empathy for his situation.

Interpretation. "I suppose each type of maintenance and repair request has to be handled in a different manner, by different people, with different equipment, and so on. That must make your job complex."

Interpretations are good because they demonstrate that you are trying to think along with the interviewee, and that the interview is not going to be just a one-sided interrogation. However, both reflection and interpretation can be hazardous because the interviewee may just sit there and say "uh-huh" to each of your reflections and interpretations. When you get through the interview, you suddenly realize you have really just been interviewing yourself! That's what we call "leading the interview," in O.F.A. parlance. Avoid this situation by specifically asking the interviewee to correct you if your reflections and interpretations are wrong.

Self-disclosure. "Well, I had no idea there were that many different types of maintenance requests. I've got a lot to learn about this area of the organization. I'm glad I can do this interview with you."

Self-disclosures, if sincere, show that you aren't a know-it-all, you're learning too, and can instill a feeling of sharing into an interview.

Silence. Don't fear periods of silence in an interview. They give the interviewee a feeling that he will have an opportunity to say whatever he wants, at his own pace. You can even emphasize these silences by saying something such as, "Please don't say anything for a minute, Jack. You've already said some important things, and I want to write them down while they are still fresh. . . ."

Define Responsibilities of Interviewing Partners

Because two members of the O.F.A. team will conduct each interview, you should decide beforehand what each of you will do. This way you will work as a team, the interview will go smoothly, and the interviewee will be encouraged to participate freely.

Since the first partner is most familiar with the activities under review, he will do most of the questioning, and will guide the interview. As mentioned before, many interviewers find it helps to draw a general flow diagram of the activities, either before or during the interview. The flow diagram focuses the interview on the work flow, rather than on the interviewee as a person. This emphasis encourages more open and direct discussions. Furthermore, the diagram will be an excellent document for subsequent analysis. The first partner is responsible for this diagram. He also examines the reports and documents processed by the interviewee, and relates these to the work flow diagram.

The second partner is responsible for all other records of the interview. As illustrated later, he will complete the several form sheets involved in the interview, and discuss these with the interviewee as they go along.

Remember to work as a team. Although the first partner is the principal questioner, he should frequently turn to the other partner and ask if he has any additional questions. This demonstrates to the interviewee that the two of you are working as a team, and reduces any possible feeling that you are competing with each other to ask questions and gather information.

In practice, however, the separation of responsibilities is never rigidly fixed. The main thing is to work as a team, get through the interview in an orderly manner, and end up with clearly documented results.

Set Time and Place

Contact the interviewee and arrange a time and place for the meeting. Allow about two hours for an average interview. You can always schedule a supplementary discussion if more time is needed.

Try to meet in the area where the interviewee works. This way, you will have free access to records and documents. Also, you can gain a better understanding of the activities if you can see the general work environment. If the interviewee has a private office or work space, meet there. Otherwise, use a nearby conference room.

Caution. Try to hold the interview in plain sight of others in the organization. Avoid any appearance of a secret review, since the overall program will be most effective if it is understood by all.

Describe the O.F.A. Program

At the start of the actual interview, you should:

- Briefly restate the central O.F.A. program objectives, scope and general process.
- Ask the interviewee if he has any questions about the program. Answer fully and frankly. If you are unable to do so, acknowledge it, and get the answers for him later.
- Explain to the interviewee how the interview will be conducted, that is, that the partners will be working as a team, but each will have some specific responsibilities. Always encourage the interviewee to freely discuss all aspects of his work, and not limit himself just to answering your specific questions. Emphasize that the interview is not an attitude survey nor should it get into discussions of personalities.

Do not slight this introduction. It is important that the interviewee understand the program and how he fits in.

Identify Major Areas of Work

Many interviewees will find it hard to discuss their own work, and will focus on one or two recent problem activities, and possibly omit other more important parts of their work.

To overcome this, start the body of the interview by asking the interviewee to briefly outline the several (usually four to eight) major areas of work which he performs, and to rank these in order of time consumed. Then ask him to assign the approximate percentage of his total effort he devotes to each major area.

This will get the conversation going, and help ensure that no important activities are omitted, and that the interview focuses on the most important areas.

Gather Work Flow Details

Focusing on each principal area of work, ask the interviewee such questions as:

1. What are the major demands that hit you?
2. Are they all the same? If not, how are they different?
3. Are they handled differently in the work flow? How? What operations are performed for some demands, but not for others?

Once you have identified the major demands and associated work flow, continue your interview with quantitative questions:

1. What is the volume of each demand?
2. How much effort is devoted to each operation in the work flow? Some interviewees prefer to estimate their effort in hours per day, per week, or per month, percentage of total time, etc. This is unimportant, since all values can be converted to hours per month following the interview.
3. What is the total cycle time for major operations?
4. How frequently do you perform the major operations?
5. What external expenses are associated with the work flow?

As you go through the interview, continue to summarize and restate. Remember the conversational responses described earlier in this chapter and use them for a more effective interview.

Once you have identified and quantified the demands and work flow, then ask the interviewee for his observations and suggestions:

1. What aspects of the demands cause you unnecessary and unproductive work?
2. How large is this unproductive work?

3. How can we change the nature of the demands to reduce the unproductive and unnecessary work, and shorten the overall cycle time?

After summarizing the interview results, complete the meeting by asking, "Who precedes and follows you in the work flow?" and "Who else is involved in this work and perhaps should be interviewed?" This will enable you to confirm your interview plan, and change it as you go along.

Level of Interviewing — Operations or Functions. The typical O.F.A. interview gathers data on work flow in terms of operations, the basic element. Later, during the analysis step, these data are summarized and categorized by function, the broader element of work flow used in analysis and improvement.

However, in some interviews, detailed operations cannot be identified, or it is not worthwhile to do so. In these cases, collect data on work flow directly at the functional rather than the operation level. Indeed, in some cases, parts of the interview will be at an operational level, and parts at the functional level.

Typically, the higher the interviewee is on the organizational ladder, or the less routine and repetitive the work is, the greater the need to interview at the functional level.

Review and Organize Interview Records

During the interview you will take pages of notes, collect documents, fill out several information follow-up sheets and key observation sheets, described later. Because of the brisk pace of the typical interview, and the fact you were engrossed in the subject, much of this documentation may be rough. Immediately after the interview, sit down with your interview partner and examine this material:

- *Review the interview data sheets* (Figure 9.2). Make sure they are clean, and that the major operations are clearly listed. Notes and data on scratch sheets should be consolidated and summarized on interview data sheets. Clip all supporting notes to these sheets.

THE
BUMBARGER
GROUP

OPERATION FUNCTION ANALYSIS   INTERVIEW DATA SHEET

NAME_____ ORGANIZATION _____ DATE_____

OPER NO	OPERATION DESCRIPTION	EFFORT	EXPENSE	CYCLE

YOUR NAME_____

Figure 9.2

- *Examine the sample reports.* Make sure you understand their source and disposition, and that you have a document and report Sheet (Figure 9.3) on each one. Remember that a "report" may be a display on a video screen.

DOCUMENT AND REPORT RECORD

THE
BUMBARGER
GROUP

DOCUMENT NAME_____

_____

DOCUMENT NUMBER/DATE_____
FREQUENCY_____
ISSUED BY_____
RECEIVED BY_____

_____

_____

_____

PRECEDING INFORMATION FLOW_____

_____

_____

_____

_____

GENERAL PURPOSE OF DOCUMENT, COMMENTS, QUESTIONS_____

_____

_____

_____

_____

_____

_____

_____

_____

Figure 9.3

- *Sort information follow-up sheets* (Figure 9.4). Keep those that you plan to use, and pass the remainder to other O.F.A. team members.
- *Review key observation sheets* (Figure 9.5). Are there other key observations that you can now recognize, and for which

you should prepare additional sheets? Remember, use one sheet for each observation.

- *Place all materials in a single interview folder* for later use in the information analysis steps.
- *Finally, arrange for any changes* in the interview list which result from this interview.

THE
BUMBARGER
GROUP

OPERATION FUNCTION ANALYSIS

INFORMATION FOLLOW-UP SHEET

ORGANIZATION_____ FUNCTION_____

REQUIRED INFORMATION   RESPONSE

RETURN TO:_____   DATE:_____

Figure 9.4

OPERATION FUNCTION ANALYSIS

KEY OBSERVATION SHEET

ORGANIZATION: _____

FUNCTIONS: _____

OBSERVATION: _____

_____

_____

_____

_____

_____

_____

_____

_____

_____

_____

_____

_____

_____

_____

_____

_____

_____

_____

_____

NAME: _____   DATE: _____

KEY OBSERVATIONS ⟹ CONCLUSIONS ⟹ RECOMMENDATIONS ⟹ IMPROVEMENTS

Figure 9.5

Interviewing — An Example

Two members of our O.F.A. team, John Goldsmith and Hank Burbank, are scheduled to interview Louise Sisk, supervisor of scheduling for the customer service department.

John works elsewhere in the customer service organization and knows something about Louise's general responsibilities, and Hank is from the in-house sales department, which has a number of interfaces with customer service. They have decided beforehand that John will lead the interview, and Hank will handle the recording.

They are in Louise's office. Let's listen in as John begins the interview.

Introduce The O.F.A. Program

John: Thanks a lot for meeting with us, Louise. Did you see the announcement by Max Harper, our general manager, about our O.F.A. program? [Shows copy.]

Louise: Yes I did, but I passed it on to others in my group. Let me see it again, please. May I keep this?

John: Sure, and we can get you some more copies for others if you wish.

As Max says here, there is a great need to become more productive in these times, and he has listed some of the major objectives of the program. Notice that this program will focus on the work flow and the activities within it. Our interview will not be an attitude survey, nor do we want to get into personality situations, or that sort of thing. Any questions so far?

Louise: Is this going to be the same sort of thing as that big efficiency drive they had about four years ago?

John: No, last time we used outside consultants who came in and did the whole thing for us; this time we're going to do it ourselves.

We've formed an O.F.A. team made of people from all parts of the organization, and Hank and I are members of it. The team is going to conduct most of the program, with help from people like you throughout the organization. We're going to conduct a lot of interviews to gather data on the activities throughout the business, as well as ideas on how to become more productive. Before we're through, we expect to get ideas from over one hundred interviews throughout the organization. Do you have any more questions about this process?

Louise: It sounds as if you're trying to get each person to speed up and work harder. Maybe it's possible, but it seems to me like most people are working pretty hard right now. Some of us have been in here for the last two Saturdays — on our own time, too. I don't see how we can work much harder than that!

John: Well, again, Louise, this is a different approach. We agree that most everyone is working good and hard. But is all that work really necessary? What do you think?

Louise: Well, I've often wondered about it. But I get all of these requests in for service work, all different types. I have to schedule them. And whenever I just about get caught up, someone else calls to check on their special request, and I have to lay everything aside and look into that one order. Then on top of that I have to issue all these reports, some regular and a lot special. At times I think people ask me to do a hundred different things every day! Those safety and housekeeping committee meetings take a lot of time, too. . . .

John: That's interesting, Louise, because in the O.F.A. language, we call all those requests for work *demands*. A person in your position can be hit by dozens of different types of demands in a period of a week. Here, this picture shows what I mean. [John opens book and shows Louise Figure 5.1.]

Every demand causes you to do work. Sometimes these demands force you to do unnecessary work. During our interview with you, we want to talk about the work you and your associates do, about the demands that force you to do this work. We want you to tell us what aspects or characteristics of these demands cause you to do what you think is unnecessary work, and together we want to find out how we can change these demands, eliminate this unnecessary work, and make this whole organization more productive.

Louise, we've all heard the old cliché, "We want to work smarter, not harder." Well, there's a lot of truth to that still. Does this make sense to you?

Louise: Well, I guess so. What did you want to know about our work here?

Describe the Interview Process

John: First, let me describe how we're going to conduct this interview. I'm going to ask most of the questions and do most of the talking with you. Hank will take most of the notes, and will pick up the questions I miss. Hank will use several form sheets as he takes his notes and he'll describe them now so you'll understand what he's doing.

Hank: The first form sheet we'll use is the interview data sheet [Figure 9.2]. As you and John discuss your activities, I'll list on this sheet the major operations you perform as you do your day-by-day work.

Louise: Do you want me to tell you how the work is *supposed* to be done, according to the standard procedures, or how we *actually* do it? Which answer do you want? You know yourself that they often aren't the same.

Hank: That's a good question, Louise. We want to know how it really happens. There are no right or wrong answers in this interview. Just tell it like it is. I'm sure no one knows more about it than you do, and that's why we're here.

Let me describe the rest of the interview data sheet. Over on the right side, we'll record your best estimate of the effort you devote to each major operation, in hours per month, as well as any external expenses that are associated with each operation, and the cycle time where that is significant. OK so far?

Louise: Sure, but I have no way to estimate some of those things. We'll be in a mess trying to do that!

Hank: Well, we have some ideas on how to do it, and we'll get to those a little later.

Now here's the second sheet we'll use, the document and report record [Figure 9.3]. I'm sure you receive and issue a lot of reports. They are important because many of them are the demands we talked about, either demands on you, or demands you place on someone else. Every time you and John talk about one of these reports, I'll fill out a document and report record on it, and if you can give us a copy of the report, we'll clip this form sheet to it.

Louise: I surely handle a lot of reports...I hope you brought a lot of those forms!

By the way. Much of the information that I used to get through printed reports, I now get through this new computer system we put in a few months ago. For example, I don't get that old service request status report anymore. I just punch the right keys and the status of each request is displayed right here on my video screen. How do you want to handle that?

Hank: Good point. I should have mentioned that. For purposes of this review, we'll consider such video displays as just another form of report, and we'll want to fill in a document and report sheet on each such display, too. Any other questions on that?

Louise: No, sounds reasonable.

Hank: Fine. This is the third form we use, the information follow-up sheet [Figure 9.4]. A number of times in this interview, you probably will mention an interface or relationship you have with another person, either in your department, or elsewhere. This person may place major demands on you, or vice versa.

In many cases, we will want to get additional information directly from these other people. In such a situation, I'll note down the required information, and then follow up later with that person.

Sometimes John and I will follow up, but in other cases we will give this sheet to another O.F.A. team member who will be interviewing that person. When they have filled in the requested information, they'll send us a copy of the completed information follow-up sheet. Do you have any questions about this sheet, Louise?

Louise: No, I'm still with you.

Hank: The fourth sheet we'll use in this interview — and throughout the whole O.F.A. program for that matter — is the key observation sheet [Figure 9.5].

Many times during this program, starting right now during this interview, someone will think of an idea. It may be a special problem associated with their work, or an unanswered question, or a potential improvement. We call these key observations. Whenever anyone thinks of one, we want to immediately write it down and keep it. Hundreds of these key observations will be gathered during this program. Later, the O.F.A. team members will sort them out, analyze them, and use them as a major input to their final conclusions and recommendations.

Louise: Did you say "conclusions and recommendations?" Are you going to report what I say here back to someone else? I better watch out what I'm saying then!

Hank: To answer your first question, yes, there will be conclusions and recommendations, and the O.F.A. team members will present these to Max Harper and his senior managers. But any information you give us, either numbers or key observations, will be added in with information we get from one hundred other interviews, so Max and his senior managers won't know where any specific piece of information came from.

On the other hand, if you come up with a key observation that leads to a strong, positive improvement recommendation, your name will stay attached to it, and you'll get the full credit for it.

John: Unless you have some more questions, Louise, let's look at this flow diagram we brought along. This shows our idea of how the work flows through this part of the business, and we would like to discuss it with you, and ask you to help us fill in some more information on it.

Louise: Hm, that looks the same as the computer diagrams that my daughter made for her courses at the university. Looks really complex to me!

John: In fact, it is pretty simple. There are only seven different symbols on the diagram, and they are summarized on this page [Figure 9.6]. Notice that the first symbol represents a person or organization, and there are a lot of those on the diagram. The next symbol stands for an information input, which often is a demand. The next symbol is a major operation in the work flow. It can be either a manual operation or a computer operation.

The fourth symbol stands for a logical decision in the process. For instance, at that point, some orders might be sent to engineering, while others pass straight on through. The next symbol is for a document or report, which also often may be a demand. Remember that a report can be in many forms, usually either a printed document

OPERATION FUNCTION ANALYSIS

WORK FLOW DIAGRAM SYMBOLS

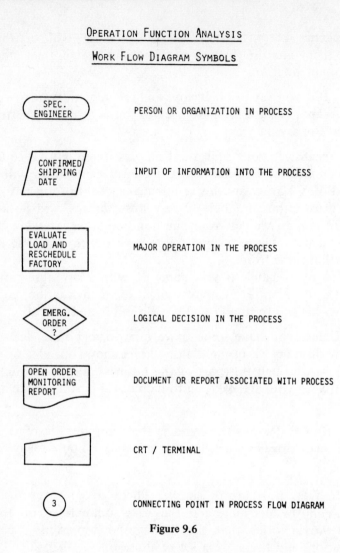

SPEC. ENGINEER	PERSON OR ORGANIZATION IN PROCESS
CONFIRMED SHIPPING DATE	INPUT OF INFORMATION INTO THE PROCESS
EVALUATE LOAD AND RESCHEDULE FACTORY	MAJOR OPERATION IN THE PROCESS
EMERG. ORDER ?	LOGICAL DECISION IN THE PROCESS
OPEN ORDER MONITORING REPORT	DOCUMENT OR REPORT ASSOCIATED WITH PROCESS
	CRT / TERMINAL
3	CONNECTING POINT IN PROCESS FLOW DIAGRAM

Figure 9.6

or a video display. The sixth symbol represents a CRT video display terminal. Although these aren't computer system diagrams, we include that symbol because so many people, like you, enter and receive much of their information through terminals, and they have become a regular part of our lives. And the last symbol is a connection point from one part of the diagram to another.

Louise: It looks like the flow diagram is just a network of all these symbols, tied together to show the work flow.

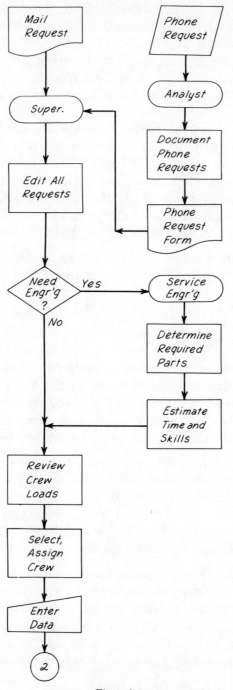

Figure 9.7

John: That's right, Louise. Let's look at the first page of this diagram Hank and I made (Figure 9.7). As we understand it, your organization receives two types of service requests, mail and telephone. After the analyst documents the phone requests, you edit all of them and decide whether or not any of them require further engineering review. If they do, you send them to service engineering, where specialists review the product engineering records, determine the required parts, estimate the required service time and skills, and then return the request to you. For each request, you review the current load on the service crews, decide which crew can best handle the request, assign the request to that crew, and then log all the information into the computer system. As shown at the bottom of the diagram, the flow then continues on page two of the diagram, and on down through these other pages we have. Does this make sense?

Louise: It sure does, but a lot of things are missing. For example, we get a lot of emergency breakdown requests, and we have to take those —

Identify Major Areas of Work

John: Excuse me for interrupting, Louise, but rather than going into the details of your work right now, can we block out your work into a half dozen or so major areas, sort of an overview of the principal functions you perform? May I write them down on the easel page over here? What is the first major area of work you have?

Louise: The main thing I do is to schedule the service requests. That's why I'm here! I spend a lot of time on that. I have to figure out what kind of equipment is involved, where it is located, what needs to be done to it. Then I figure out which service team can handle it, about how long they will need. Once I decide this, I enter the request into my terminal . . . Here, let me show you how —

John: Excuse me for interrupting, Louise, but we'll come back later in the interview for some of these details. Right now let's focus on our list of major areas of effort. Sounds as if you've hit one. Let's call it a function, and name it service request scheduling. OK? Let me write it down on the easel so we can all see it. Louise, how much of your time do you think you spend on service request scheduling?

Louise: I haven't the foggiest idea. It can vary all over the place. I spent most of yesterday doing it, but I won't get to any of it today. I don't know. It could vary from zero to one hundred percent!

John: How much would it be for an average month?

Louise: I still can't say. I would be glad to keep some log sheets for the next few months, and tell you then, but I honestly can't say sitting here right now. No matter what I would say, it would be wrong. Someone would check on it, find I was off, and then jump all over me. I know how it is when it comes to making estimates of time!

John: Don't worry about estimating the time right now, we'll come back to that later. And you won't have to worry about people second guessing your estimates of effort, for two reasons. First, no one knows more about it than you, so you're the best one to make the estimate. Second, your estimates will be combined with the estimates of a number of other people, so it will be hard to pull yours out and pick on it individually.

Let's think about the next big block of work. What would that be?

Louise: Reports! Somehow I seem to spend hours each week preparing reports. Some of them are regular reports, and some are specials. I make them for all sorts of reasons! I've laid out some of them. Want to see them now?

John: Let's not get into them right now. But that can be a big job for sure. Later we'll want to list down all of the reasons for these reports, but for now let's just lump them into a function called service request reporting. How does that sound?

Louise: Fine with me. I suppose that we could call it anything we wanted, as long as we all agree on the name.

John: That's right. Let me write it here on the easel. What's the next major responsibility you have?

Louise: Well, one of the worst parts of my job is to make out the annual budget for the department. For some reason, Mike Gerriton, our department manager, gave me this assignment over four years ago, before I took over the scheduling job, and I'm still stuck with it. I guess we should call it department budgeting. It's a real drag. For the last two weeks, I've devoted every spare moment to it — a real burden. I had to lay aside a lot of my regular work for it. Some of those customers really got mad.

John: Why did the customers get mad at you for preparing the department budget?

Louise: Because I couldn't take time to follow up on their requests. I guess this leads me to the next major thing I do. I spend a lot of time checking up on the status of the service requests — more than I should, I guess. But everyone calls me to find out what's happening to their service request.

Who knows? I have to call all over the place to find out. And by the time I finally find out the status, and call the customer back — well, by then the status has changed again!

Customers, field sales reps, our own marketing people — they're all mad at me. [Hank is filling out a key observation sheet on this as Louise talks, and also some information follow-up sheets to remind them to check with these others on this same problem to evaluate its seriousness.]

John: That sounds like another good one. Let me write it down here on the easel. What should we call it?

Louise: Well, I guess we could call it service request follow-up and monitoring. That's what it is.

John: Fine. What's the next one?

Louise: Well, I forgot one of the most important ones until right now.

The first thing I do when I receive service requests — even before I schedule them — is to look at them to be sure they are right. You know, we get a lot of requests that should not even come here — should go to another division of the company, for instance. Often major pieces of information are completely missing, or there are obvious errors in the request.

I check through this and make sure the service request is clear before I start it through the process.

John: I can see that would be important. What should we call that function? How about service request editing? By the way, do you do all the work on these service requests? That is, all the scheduling, follow up, and editing?

Louise: George, my assistant does some. He handles the editing on requests for those three new product lines we have. You know, the ones that came out last year. He helps some with the follow up, and the foremen of the service crews spend a lot of time on that, too. [Hank fills out information follow-up sheets on this as a reminder to discuss this with George and the foremen at a later time.]

John: That's an impressive looking list. Anything else to add to it?

Louise: There are lots of other odds and ends, administrative type of work, I guess you'd call it. Every six months I make out performance reports on George and five others here in the department. I'm our department's representative on the safety and housekeeping committee. Mr. Harper asked me to head up that new equal opportunity task force in the division. Lot's of things like that. I suppose you could call all that type of work something like general administration.

John: Sounds good to me. We can dig back into it later for some of the detail if we want to. Are you reasonably satisfied with the list now, Louise? If we've missed anything major we can always add it later.

Louise: Looks OK to me.

John: Now I know it's very hard to accurately estimate how much time you spend on each of these major functions, but let's try to list them in order of size. Think back over the past six months or so. Which one did you spend the most time doing?

Louise: Well, I guess I spent the most time over the past six months or a year on the service order follow-up and monitoring. I hate to admit it, and my manager would die if he knew it, but that's how it is.

John: Great. Remember, there are no right or wrong answers in this interview. We aren't interested in how things are *supposed* to be, only how they really are!

What is the next largest block of effort, and from there on down?

Louise: Hm . . . I guess the next one would be the service request editing, then the scheduling, then the reports, budgeting, and administration — in that order.

John: Good. Let me get them written down in that order. Now I'm going to ask you to do what you said was impossible a few minutes ago — estimate the amount of effort devoted to each of these activities.

Let's try this. If you weren't here, Louise, and Hank and I had to do it ourselves, we would look at that list, see six functions, and have to assume that you spend an equal amount of time on each. That is . . . let's see . . . a little under seventeen percent on each function.

Now we all know that wouldn't be right. You can do better than Hank and I can. Sometimes it is easiest to estimate some of the smaller functions. How much time in an average month do you think you spend on the general administration function?

Louise: Oh, let's see. I suppose I spend a couple of hours a week, one way or the other on it. Maybe a bit more. Put down three hours a week. What percentage would that be?

Hank: Well, assuming a forty hour week, that would be about seven and a half percent. Sound about right Louise?

Louise: I guess so. I would think it would be less than ten percent.

John: How about the function of department budgeting? How much effort on that?

Louise: Well, it's sort of a once a year event, now that I think of it. I suppose it takes up about half of my time for about three weeks out of the year. No more than that.

Hank: Let's see. That would be about one and a half weeks per year. If we assume about forty-eight weeks a year, based on four weeks of vacations, holidays, and so forth . . . That means you devote about three percent of your time — over a period of a year — to department budgeting. How does that sound?

Louise: I would have thought it was more than that, but your way of figuring is reasonable. I guess it just seemed more important to me because I have been working on it recently. I suppose you should change the order of the last two functions on the easel. Put department budgeting with three percent last, and general administrative next to last with eight percent.

John: Fine. Those two total eleven percent. That leaves eighty-nine percent to distribute over the remaining four functions. How do you think we should spread that, Louise? For instance, does the first one up there, service order follow-up, is it half of that 89 percent?

Louise: No, it wouldn't be that large. Let me see . . . I guess it is about a third, and the others are about equal. What does that figure out to be?

Hank: Let's see . . . That means that service order follow-up and monitoring consumes about thirty percent of your total effort, and editing, scheduling, and reporting each consume about twenty percent.

Gather Work Flow Details

John: Good enough, this means that all four are big and important, and we should talk about all four of them. If we can get to the other two, we will. Otherwise, we might have to come back later.

Let's talk about these four in their general sequence. Let's begin with service request editing. Tell us how that's done. What are the main demands that cause you to do this work? What operations are performed to meet these demands? I suppose it begins when you get the request for service? How do you get these requests?

Louise: Well, there really are three main ways I get those service requests. Most by telephone, some by telex, and some by letters.

John: Hank is going to start to write this information down on his interview data sheets, and I'm going to refine our flow diagram as you talk. There are no secrets here, so feel free to look over our shoulders and be sure we get the right information recorded.

Let me put the input symbols at the top of the flow diagram to represent the three different types of service requests, one document symbol for the telexes, one document symbol for the letters, and one information input symbol for the telephone messages.

Can you estimate how many requests you receive a month by each way?

Louise: Actually, we're lucky there. We keep this log of all requests, and I can check down through the past few months and average out some numbers for you. Shall I do that now?

John: Not right now. You can do that after the interview, and Hank or I can get it from you. Do you handle all three types of requests the same way when you do the editing?

Louise: Well, the telexes and letters are about the same, but the telephone requests are different. I have to do more work on them. I have to fill in this form sheet we have here, a telephone request form.

Hank: May I have a copy of that? Let me attach a document and report record sheet to that. We may get some more details on it later.

John: Louise, do all three types of service requests require about the same amount of effort to edit?

Louise: Oh, no. The phone requests take more time to receive and write down. We don't have to do any of that with the other two types of requests.

On the other hand, when a customer calls us we can ask him the necessary questions right on the spot, and get the information the first time. On the telex and letter requests, we sometimes have to go back for additional information, and corrections. That part takes a lot longer.

Incidentally, I just thought of something when I mentioned the word customer. We get all three types of requests from three sources, too. Some come from our distributors, some from our sales reps, and many directly from the customers.

John: Hmm, I'd better change my flow diagram to show that. Hank, did you get that down? This gets complex. Louise, does the source of the request influence the amount of editing you have to do? In other words, does a telephone request from a sales rep take the same editing effort as one from a distributor, or one from a customer?

Louise: No, they're not the same. The ones directly from the customers are the toughest, because they don't know exactly what information we need to do the right servicing job. The ones from the distributors are the easiest, and the ones from the sales reps are in between.

John: Well, this really is complex. I guess we had better trace each type of service request, from each source right through the processing. Many operations will be the same, I'm sure, but will require different times. Hank will get those down on his sheets. I suppose that each type of request will have certain operations unique to it, too?

Louise, let's start with the request you receive most often. Which would that be? Just start at the beginning and tell us how you handle them. Not every little detail, but the major operations within the editing area.

Louise: I'll get the exact number for you later, but I'm sure that the largest volume of requests are the telephone requests received directly from the customers. When we get one of those the first thing I do is to. . . .

Well, the interview is underway. It may seem that John and Hank spent a lot of time introducing the program to Louise, and describing the interviewing process, form sheets, etc., but they were able to put Louise at ease, and launch a good interview.

Typically, Louise wanted to get right into the details of her work. John and Hank correctly kept her off these until they first established the major activities, in fact, the four major functions Louise performed.

Louise choked up, as nearly always happens, when John first mentioned the subject of estimates. He wisely did not push it, but glided into the subject later, helping Louise make her first estimates of the time devoted to each major function. After that, the ice was broken; Louise found she could make the estimates, and that she was the best one to do it.

Notice that Louise did not describe her big functions first. People often start talking about the things they think they should emphasize, or the things that have hurt them most recently. Louise did both. She is the supervisor of scheduling for service request, so she's sure she should mention that first, regardless of how much time she actually spends on that task.

Since she is sick and tired of making reports, she mentions that next. And then because she just went through the annual budget battle, she lists that next!

Once John and Hank had guided Louise into defining her major duties, they then focused on the largest block of work.

John and Hank are nearly through with their interview with Louise. She has described how she performs the four main functions. Hank has listed the major operations for each function on the interview data sheets, along with estimates of hours per month of effort, external expenses, and cycle times where significant. They have gathered estimates on the volume and frequency of major demands. John has added some details to his flow diagram.

They have not talked about operations in the two smallest functions, general administration and department budgeting, for two reasons. First, they consume only a small amount of Louise's total effort, and second, time is running out!

Let's go back and listen in on the end of their interview.

Interview Finale — The Best Part

John: Louise, this has been great. You have given us some important information. You probably have noticed that Hank has filled out several key observation sheets. Hank, what do you have down there?

Hank: Well, the first key observation reads this way. . . . [Hank reads off the several sheets he has completed.]

John: Louise, I'm sure you have some more key observations. Is there anything we haven't talked about? Any ideas of unnecessary effort you see around here, ways we could change some of the demands we've talked about, ways we could run this business better?

Louise: Well, one thing I have always wondered about is why we have to. . . .

Now Louise gets to the best part of the interview: the last ten minutes, when the best ideas come out. John and Hank get them down on the key observation sheets, and the interview draws to a close.

John: Louise, thank's a lot for this help. You've been great. We understand some of the ideas you gave us are sort of confidential, and we won't emphasize where we got them. However, that one idea you had about a better way to handle those telex and letter service requests sounds great. It could save considerable time in several areas, and best of all, it would increase customer satisfaction. We'd like to give you credit for that when we put it in the final report to the senior managers? OK?

Louise: Well, sure. I appreciate that.

Hank: When you get the demand volume information, give it to either of us. If possible, by the end of the week.

John: Louise, are there others involved in these activities you think we should talk to? Here's our list of interviewees. What do you think?

Louise: Well, the only one I can think of is Willis Fullerton. He's over in the supply department. We work closely with him on integrating the service requests schedules with the supply schedules. You may want to talk with him.

John: Sounds like a good idea. We'll check with him. Thanks again — we appreciate your help.

SUMMARY

Phase 2 begins with the O.F.A. team training and planning. The team members prepare their overall work plan and refine the objectives and scope of the program.

They then focus on the information collection process. They decide who should be interviewed, assign the interviews to team members, and then establish their final Phase 2 schedule.

This chapter has shown the need for information collection and has illustrated the interviewing process by which you collect this information.

Chapter 10
Information Analysis

Through the information collection steps described in the preceding chapter, you will gather information on the activities within your organization. However, before you can draw conclusions and make recommendations, you must analyze this information, as illustrated in Figure 10.1 and described in detail in this chapter.

In this analysis process, you will consolidate the data on operation summary sheets, sort and categorize it on function summary sheets, and further consolidate it on the O.F.A. ratio summary sheets. At the same time, key observations obtained during information collection are reviewed, analyzed and consolidated. Taken together, the quantitative data and the key observations then form the basis for the subsequent conclusions and recommendations.

To help conduct this analysis, the O.F.A. team should select three of its members for special assignments within the team:

1. One person to maintain the master lists and definitions of functions and demands, and the demand volumes
2. One person to coordinate and maintain the analysis summary sheets
3. One person to collect, sort, and analyze the key observation sheets.

With this background, let's go through the analysis process step by step.

OPERATION SUMMARY SHEETS

Organize Operation Summary Sheets

Information gathered during your interviews will be scattered over dozens of interview data sheets (Figure 9.2) and many supporting documents, all filed in folders at the time of the interviews.

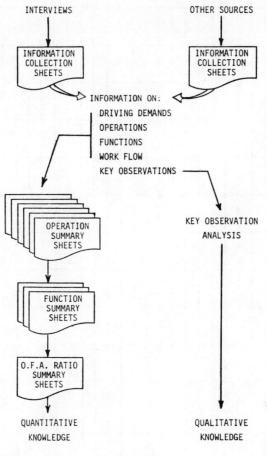

Figure 10.1

Each two-person team now will gather this information from their own interviews, and post it on the operation summary sheets, using a separate sheet for each group of people.

For example, you may have interviewed several people in the inventory control area. You will post the interview results for these people on one operation summary sheet (with overflow to other sheets as necessary), with "Inventory Control" written in the activities label in the upper right corner of the sheet (Figure 10.2).

Next, enter the names of the interviewees from this group in the column headings. If the interviewee's work is essentially unique, and

OPERATION FUNCTION ANALYSIS

OPERATION SUMMARY SHEET

ACTIVITIES:

OPER NO	OPERATION DESCRIPTION	FUNCTION DESCRIPTION	DEMAND DESCRIPTION	TOTAL									

THE BUMBARGER GROUP. / Atlanta

Figure 10.2

he alone does it, then enter his name in the column heading. If his work is typical of several other people, and he "represents," say, three other people as well, then place the note "(4)" in the column heading next to the interviewee's name to clearly indicate that the data in the column is for a total of four people. If it is a group interview, label the column heading with the name of the group and the number of people involved, e.g., "Material Stock Pickers (4)."

Enter Interview Data

Arrange the interview folders for this set of activities in the general order of work flow. Review the interview data sheets from the first interview. Clearly identify the operations performed by this interviewee. Make sure that all time is accounted for, that is, that the hours recorded total the number of man-hours in a month, say 160.

Next, list these operations on the operation summary sheet, in the column headed "Operation Description." Skip lines so you will have room to insert operations which you may identify later. If all or part of the interview was conducted on a functional rather than an operational basis, as described in Chapter 9, the appropriate *functions* should be listed in the operation description column, instead of the operations.

For each operation (or function) listed in the operation description column, enter the hours from the interview data sheet in the column under that interviewee's name. Remember that if the interviewee "represents" several people, or if it is a group interview, the hours entered into the column should represent the time for the total group.

Repeat this process for all of your interviews. If you find that a later interviewee performs some of the same operations as an earlier interviewee, place these operations on the same line on the operation summary sheet.

Your O.F.A. team leader will assign a block of operation numbers to each two-person interviewing team, and you will then assign a number to each operation (or function) listed in the operation description column on the operation summary sheet.

Identify Functions and Demands

Chapter 6 describes the relationship between functions and operations. That is, each function is composed of a number of smaller operations.

One of the first steps you did in the information collection process, as described in Chapter 9, was to prepare a master list of principal functions. Get that list now. Review each operation summary sheet and identify and enter in the column headed "Function Description" the function that relates to each operation shown there.

If all or part of the interview was conducted on a functional rather than operational level, the function name will now appear in both the operation and function description columns.

Many of these functions will be on your master list. However, you always will find certain operations that do not relate to any functions on your list. In this case, simply create and define a new function.

Report your new functions to the team member who is the keeper of the list. He then can update the list and distribute copies to all O.F.A. team members. In this way, the master list is automatically refined during the analysis process, and all team members will use the same function definitions.

Finally, enter the name of the driving demand associated with each operation, that is, the demand that causes the interviewee to perform that operation. Remember that you may not be able to identify a demand for each operation. Some may be recognized later, some never. If you identify any new demands, submit them to the person responsible for the functions and demands lists so he can keep these lists up to date. Give him your best estimates of demand volumes so he can tabulate them on the demand volume summary sheet (Figure 10.3).

Identify Alternate Routes

Similar demands often pass through a series of operations and then reach a decision point or intersection in the process. Because of its unique characteristics, one category of demand then passes through its alternate route — that is, a series of operations performed for it — while the other category of demand passes through a different alternate route of operations. The two demands may or may not rejoin paths later in the process.

Be sure to identify these alternate routes on your operation summary sheets because much of your later evaluation and recommendation process may be based on these different routes.

OPERATION FUNCTION ANALYSIS

DEMAND VOLUME SUMMARY SHEET

SOURCES OF
ESTIMATES

DEMANDS

AVERAGE

THE
BUMBARGER
GROUP

Figure 10.3

A Typical Operation Summary Sheet

The operation summary sheet shown in Figure 10.4 illustrates several things. First, notice that this sheet was prepared for the inside sales department. The column headings indicate that the interviews recorded here covered the work of 20 people in that department. Johnson and Schmidt were single interviews, each focusing on his activities, alone. Ortega, Saunders, Botich, and Batter were interviews with a single person who represented several others as well. The three analysts were covered in a group interview, as were the four technicians.

For the sake of clear illustration, this sheet includes only five operations, each related to a different function. Usually several operations on any given sheet would relate to one function.

Let's look at each operation in Figure 10.4 and see what it shows us. The first one, Operation No. 58, is a review of pricing, terms, and conditions on customer orders. It relates to a function, order editing — commercial, and all orders pass through this operation. The three analysts, Ortega and her friend, and Saunders and his three friends all share in performing this operation, for a total of 580 man-hours per month.

Operation No. 60 is an alternate route operation. The same people now sort out the orders that have been rejected because of incomplete or inaccurate information. They then obtain this information from field sales and customers. Notice that this relates to a different function, that is, order editing — commercial — rejects, and is driven by a different demand, namely the rejected orders.

This alternate route, and the different function, are important because they give us a way to identify the extra, unnecessary effort caused by poor data on orders received from field sales. We can immediately see that the organization spends *at least* 630 man-hours per month on this unnecessary, unproductive work. There are probably additional hours on the field sales operation summary sheets, so the total time may be much more than the 630 hours shown on this sheet.

Operation No. 62 shows that the accepted orders now pass to Johnson, Schmidt, and Botich and her friend, who prepare order folders and manufacturing backlog files, for a total of 410 hours per month. This operation supports the function, order entry — manufacturing, and the driving demand is all accepted orders. Volume

OPERATION SUMMARY SHEET
ACTIVITIES: Inside Sales

OPERATION FUNCTION ANALYSIS

OPER NO	OPERATION DESCRIPTION	FUNCTION DESCRIPTION	DEMAND DESCRIPTION	TOTAL	Johnson	Schmidt	Analyst f(3)	Ortega f(2)	Saunders f(4)	Botich f(4)	Technician f(2)	Salter f(3)
58	Compare customer orders with proposals for pricing, terms and conditions. Set aside orders with missing, inaccurate info.	Order editing - Commercial	All orders	580			260	120	200			
60	Sort rejected orders by originating sales office. Obtain required info.	Order editing - Commercial - Rejects	Rejected orders	630			220	110	300			
62	Prepare order folders and manufacturing backlog files for accepted orders.	Order entry - Manufact.	Accepted orders	410	140	150				120		
64	Review orders for technical requirements	Order editing - Technical	Accepted orders	610	20	10			60	100	140	280
66	List components that require special engineering. Enter details in Engineering backlog files	Order entry - Engineering	Engineer. Orders	870				90	80	90	410	200
					160	160	480	320	640	310	550	480

THE BUMGARGER GROUP / Atlanta

Figure 10.4

may be the same as all orders, on the assumption that all rejected orders eventually get accepted, or it might be somewhat less if some orders are permanently rejected.

In Operation No. 64, many people review each order to identify which orders require special engineering, and the nature of that special engineering. This operation is related to a function, order editing – technical, and is performed on every accepted order.

Operation No. 66 is the start of a long alternate route through design engineering. This operation indicated 870 hours per month were spent listing those components that require special design engineering work, and entering these details into the engineering backlog files. The driving demand is the order that requires engineering work.

Notice two things. This operation summary sheet contains all the hours for some people, but less than all for Botich and friend, and for the four technicians. The remainder of their times will be on other operation summary sheets.

Also, any one of the functions shown on this sheet typically will receive inputs from operations on other operation summary sheets. For example, operations probably are performed in field sales which contribute to the function, order editing – commercial. Operations performed in design engineering will contribute to order entry – engineering.

FUNCTION SUMMARY SHEETS

Once you have accumulated your interview data on the operation summary sheets, you then will reduce and consolidate it first on the function summary working sheets (Figure 10.5) and then on the function summary sheets (Figure 10.6).

Organize Function Sheets

At the start of this chapter, you read that one member of the O.F.A. team would be responsible for coordinating and maintaining the analysis summary sheets, including the two mentioned above. His first task will be to organize and set up these two sheets.

Notice the columns, on both sheets, represent major departments or sections within the scope of the O.F.A. program. Therefore, he must identify and select these departments through discussions with other team members.

Figure 10.5

OPERATION FUNCTION ANALYSIS

FUNCTION SUMMARY SHEET

ACTIVITIES:

FUNC NO	FUNCTION DESCRIPTION	DEMAND DESCRIPTION	DEMAND VOLUME	ORGANIZATIONS											
				TOTAL											

THE BUMBARGER GROUP / Atlanta

Figure 10.6

Typical office, knowledge work departments in an equipment manufacturing business might be:

Market research and product planning
Field sales
Inside sales
Contract administration
Application engineering
Design engineering
Production and inventory control
Purchasing
Industrial and manufacturing engineering
Factory supervision
After-shipment service and parts
Operations accounting
Human resources

In a medium-size mortgage banking firm, the principal departments might be:

Loan origination, residential
Loan origination, commercial
Loan origination, construction
Loan conveyance, processing
Loan conveyance, closing
Secondary marketing
Loan administration, cashier
Loan administration, collection
Loan administration, insurance and taxes
Corporate accounting
Banking
Office administration

Once he has defined these departments, the team member responsible for the analysis summary sheets enters their names into the column headings on a function summary working sheet, and makes a copy for each function. He then obtains the current list of functions, list of demands, and demand volume summary sheet, and enters the name of the function, driving demand, and demand volume in the heading of each sheet. Demands not known at this time can be entered later when identified.

Caution. Remember that many functions will not have a clearly defined driving demand. It is better to omit the demand than to create an artificial demand.

Once the responsible team member has organized these working sheets, he then sets up the function summary sheets. He enters the names of the major departments into the column headings, lists the functions, and where appropriate the demands and demand volumes. He places both the function summary working sheets and the function summary sheets in a notebook, ready for the team members to enter the data.

Enter Data from Operation Sheets

Each two-person interviewing team now reviews its operation summary sheets, abstracts each operation, and enters it with its associated man-hours into the appropriate function summary working sheet. To save effort, abbreviate the operation descriptions and rely on the operation numbers for identification.

Always make sure that the driving demand shown for the operation on the operation summary sheet is the same as for the function on the function summary working sheet. If not, review your original interview notes, discuss it with others who have recorded related data on that function, and together identify the proper demand.

Recognize and clearly identify alternate routes. For example, Figure 10.4 shows two separate yet related functions, order editing – commercial and order editing – commercial – rejects. The two might have been combined into one function, order editing. However, this would have concealed the fact that at least 630 man-hours of effort are devoted each month to unnecessary, unproductive work. Indeed, all three order editing functions shown in Figure 10.4 might have been combined, further masking reality. Therefore, make sure that the list of functions is structured to expose such unnecessary work. Now is the time to add functions if necessary.

Figure 10.7 illustrates a partially complete function summary working sheet. It includes not only Operation No. 58 from the operation summary sheet shown in Figure 10.4, but also Operation No. 20, performed in field sales, from another operation summary

OPERATION FUNCTION ANALYSIS   PRINCIPAL DEMAND _All customer orders_   DEMAND VOLUME _330/month_

FUNCTION SUMMARY WORKING SHEET
FUNCTION: _Order Editing - Commercial_

OPER NO	OPERATION DESCRIPTION	ORGANIZATIONS											
		Mkt.Res.	Fld.Sales	I/s Sales	Appl.Eng.	Des.Eng.	P&I.C.	Purchas.	I.E.&M.E.	Fact.Sup.	Service	Credit	Acct'g
20	Review customer order for shipping instructions and customer data			230									
50	Compare customer order with proposals - commercial data			580									

TOTAL MAN-HOURS PER MONTH FOR THIS FUNCTION BY DEPARTMENT

TOTAL MAN-HOURS PER MONTH FOR THIS FUNCTION

THE BUMBARGER GROUP / Atlanta

Figure 10.7

sheet not shown in the example. Notice the line for totals by department, and the place for the grand total for the function.

After all two-person teams have entered their data on the function summary working sheets, the person responsible for these data sheets, with the help of others, totals all values on each working sheet, and transfers these values to the function summary sheets. A partially complete function summary sheet is shown in Figure 10.8.

O.F.A. RATIO SUMMARY SHEET

This is the final sheet used in the analysis process, and is illustrated in Figure 10.9. All functions for which you can identify a driving demand are listed on this sheet, along with the demand description and volume. You then calculate the O.F.A. ratios in total and for each contributing organization, as described in Chapter 6.

The transfer of data and calculations described above are illustrated in a simplified case in Figure 10.10.

Computer or Manual Calculations

The calculations described on the preceding pages can be performed on any modest-size computer, without the need to transfer data manually from one set of sheets to another.

Use of a computer has one major advantage. You can enter new and changed data at any time during the analysis process and immediately see the results and impact of these changes. Operations can be added or deleted. Demand volumes can be added or changed. Relationships between operations and functions can be changed. It is a great convenience, and ensures that the calculations are accurate.

On the other hand, the use of the manual sheets described above has a major advantage. As you enter, add, and transfer these numbers through the sheets, you will automatically think about them, test and evaluate their reasonableness, and reflect on their meaning and significance. As a result, you often will make new key observations based on your growing understanding of these numbers. This continual, in-process study of the data is lost if calculations are handled through a computer or by clerks not involved in the program. In any case, the size of your program, and volume of data, will influence your decision.

OPERATION FUNCTION ANALYSIS

ACTIVITIES: Order Receipt

FUNC NO	FUNCTION DESCRIPTION	DEMAND DESCRIPTION	DEMAND VOLUME	TOTAL	ORGANIZATIONS										
					MktRes	Fld.Sales	Ins.Sales	Appl.Eng	Dist.Eng	P.I.C.	Purchs	Fac.Oper	Service	Credit	Acctg
	Market Forecasting	—		680	320	180	60	80	40						
	Price Policy Administr.	—		180			180								
	Sales Development	—		980		760	220								
	Direct Selling	Proposals	240	1260		1260									
	Proposal Preparation	Proposals	940	2730		360	1120	640	110						
	Order Editing-Commer.	All Orders	330	810		230	580								
	Ovd.Edit-Comm.Rejects	Reject Ord's	60	1040		410	630								
	Ovr.Edit-Technical	Accepted Ord's	310	880		90	610	120	60						
	Order Entry-Manufac.	Accep.Orders	310	500			410			90					
	Order Entry-Eng'g	Eng'd Orders	290	1050		870	140	40							
	Order Follow-Up	Accep.Orders	310	1370			170			940		260			
	Advance-Engrg	Eng'd Orders	290	1550				730	820						
	Production Engrg	Eng'd Orders	290	2850				150	2700						
	Manufact. Planning	Accep. Order	310	500						340		160			
	Production Control	Parts Released	270M	1250						880		370			

Figure 10.8

THE BURBARGER GROUP / Atlanta

Figure 10.9

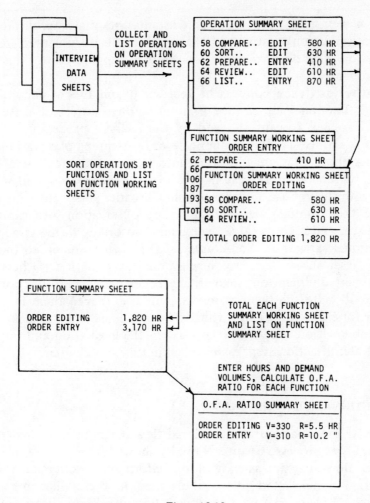

Figure 10.10

KEY OBSERVATIONS

Earlier in this chapter, we mentioned three O.F.A. team members with special responsibilities. You've read about the first two: one responsible for the function and demand lists, and the other for the data summary sheets. The third person is responsible for organizing the key observations.

Throughout the information collection process and even the entire program, both the interviewees and the O.F.A. team members will gain new insights into the problems and potential improvements in the organization's activities. These should be documented immediately on key observation sheets, and a copy given to this third team member.

He reviews each copy as he receives it and files it according to broad functional areas. (See Chapter 6 for examples of these functional areas.) Toward the end of the analysis process, he reviews them again. He combines duplicate or overlapping observations, and divides those that are too broad into two or more specific observations. Often it works best if one or two other team members help him with this review, in order to gain a broader perspective.

He then summarizes each final key observation into a one-line sentence, and records these "one-liners" according to the same broad functional categories. Some users of O.F.A. have recorded these on large easel sheets for easy display and examination. Others have documented them on smaller sheets for easy reproduction and distribution to the team members. One user placed them in a computer for easier filing and sorting. The one-liners and the background key observation sheets will be used in the evaluation and improvement identification step, as described in the next chapter.

FUNCTIONAL FLOW DIAGRAMS

Many O.F.A. teams draw functional flow diagrams as a final step in the analysis process. Chapter 9 briefly showed how to draw an *operational* flow diagram as part of the information collection process. Figure 9.6 illustrated the symbols used in these diagrams. These same symbols can be used to draw a *functional* flow diagram except that the third symbol in Figure 9.6 is used to represent a function, rather than an operation.

Figure 10.11 shows a small portion of a functional flow diagram. Notice the data on man-hours per month devoted to each function, and demand volumes per month. Other notes, data on O.F.A. ratios, etc., typically are added to the diagram.

Notice, too, the alternate route for the rejected customer orders, and the 20 orders a month that are permanently rejected and returned to the customers. The diagram also shows the beginning of the alternate route through engineering, for 90 orders a month, while

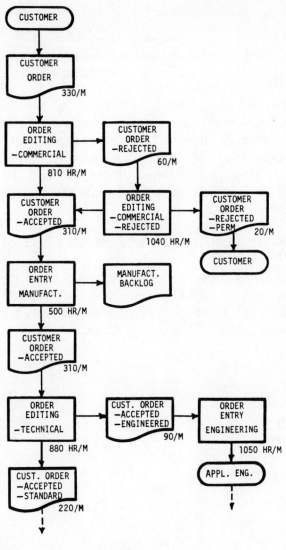

Figure 10.11

220 "standard" orders a month pass directly into the downstream processes.

Functional flow diagrams and their data are used during the subsequent evaluation and improvement identification process, and in the presentation of final results to the senior managers.

SUMMARY

The information you gathered during the information collection step is raw, and must be analyzed and consolidated before you can use it to draw conclusions and make recommendations. This chapter described how to do this.

Original data on operations performed by the interviewees are abstracted from the interview data sheets and tabulated on the operation summary sheets. This information then is sorted by function, and placed on the function summary working sheets, from which it is further consolidated on the function summary sheets. O.F.A. ratios are calculated as appropriate and posted on the O.F.A. ratio summary sheets.

Key observation sheets are sorted according to major functional areas, combined and divided as appropriate and condensed into one-liners.

Functional flow diagrams often are prepared as the final step in the analysis process, and they, along with the statistical data and key observations, are used in the evaluation and improvement recommendation process described in the next chapter.

Chapter 11
Evaluation and
Improvement Identification

At this point in the O.F.A. process, you have collected and analyzed quantitative data as well as qualitative key observations on the activities in your organization. Now you are going to:

- Evaluate this information, try to make sense out of it, and see what it really means
- Based on this evaluation, identify potential improvements and changes in the activities and work flow that will make your organization more productive.

This evaluation and improvement identification is especially challenging because you must shift from an analytical mode to a creative and innovative mode. You must become curious, creative, audacious, even impertinent, all characteristics our families, schools, and jobs knocked out of us years ago. Remember what Henry Kissenger said, "Ask an impertinent question, get a pertinent answer." Don't hesitate to ask innovative questions you never dared ask before.

Chapter 3 presented some of the common obstacles to innovation. Chapter 4 described how we can develop and use creative skills and attitudes to overcome these obstacles. Go back now and review these two chapters, and you will be in a better position to carry out the process described in the following sections.

PRODUCTIVITY IMPROVEMENT TEAMS

For purposes of evaluation and improvement identification, the full O.F.A. team now breaks into several smaller groups, often called *improvement teams.* Each improvement team will focus on a major area of the organization. In some cases, an improvement team may consist of a single, two-person interviewing team. Another might consist of two or more interviewing teams.

For instance, in an equipment manufacturing business, an improvement team may focus on the materials planning and control processes, and could consist of three interviewing teams: the one for production planning, the one for purchasing, and the one for inventory control. In a mortgage banking firm, an improvement team might concentrate on all loan origination activities, and would include the interviewing teams responsible for residential, commercial, and construction loans.

These improvement teams are not fixed. Part way through the evaluation and improvement identification process, you may recognize a need for additional work. If this happens, establish another improvement team.

EVALUATION

Review Key Observations

In Chapter 10 you read about the "third person" on the O.F.A. team, who was responsible for accumulating and summarizing the key observations. One of his principal responsibilities was to condense the key observations into a list of one-liners, each summarizing a single observation, all categorized according to major functional areas.

He now will present this list to the entire O.F.A. team for their review. If anyone questions a particular observation, the person most familiar with it can fully discuss it. At the same time, all team members can expand these observations and add others. In this way, every member of the O.F.A. team gains a general understanding of all observations, and each improvement team can focus on those observations associated with its scope of activities. This general understanding of the key observations will give your whole O.F.A. team a good background for the subsequent evaluation work.

Review and Compare All Functions

There was a "second person" on the O.F.A. team, too; he was responsible for organizing the function summary sheets and related documents.

He now should prepare a condensed list showing the total man-hours devoted to each function by the whole organization.

The entire O.F.A. team should review this list. Search for the largest functions and test their reasonableness. Locate the smallest functions, too, and evaluate them. Compare related functions. What do you see?

Example

Table 11.1 is a condensed function list prepared by an O.F.A. team in a typical equipment manufacturing business. Imagine the team's reaction when they saw that their business devoted more effort to *documenting* their product designs than to *creating* these designs, by a factor of more than 4½ : 1!

> Designing the Order: 1,144 man-hours per month
> Documenting the Design: 5,436 man-hours per month
> 5,436/1,144 = 4.75

Imagine their greater consternation when they discovered for the first time (Table 11.2) that their business spent more time monitoring and expediting their customer orders than in originally scheduling them by a ratio of more than 7½ : 1!

If you think the O.F.A. team was surprised by these numbers, imagine the response of their own senior managers when they received the team's final report! Needless to say, these same senior managers initiated major improvement programs focused on the areas of order design and documentation, and process scheduling and control.

Caution. Don't brush off this example with the comment, "Oh well, that probably was a rather ineffective business. We aren't that bad for sure!" Not so. This business was:

- The most profitable division in a large, international company
- An acknowledged leader in its marketplace.

Caution. Do not make the error of focusing only on the large functions, with the hope of reducing the effort devoted to them. It

Table 11.1. Summary of Functions—Hours Per Month.

PLANNING AND DEVELOPMENT—5%

1.1	General business planning	104
1.2	Market forecasting	55
1.3	Product planning and development	866
1.4	Sales development	202
1.5	Resource planning and development	30
1.6	Financial forecasting	64
1.7	Financial planning and development	60
1.8	Manufacturing standards data development	133
1.9	Control of shop equipment needs	185
	TOTAL	1,699

GETTING THE ORDER—3%

2.4	Sales liaison	114
2.5	Direct selling	86
2.6	Product application—sales	379
2.7	Product application—engineering	198
2.8	Cost estimate	11
2.9	Order proposal	317
	TOTAL	1,105

ENTERING THE ORDER—7%

3.1	Order editing	1,057
3.2	Order entry	522
3.3	Order acknowledgment	76
3.4	Order follow-up	167
3.5	Order control and monitoring	494
	TOTAL	2,316

DESIGNING THE ORDER—3%

3.7	Order editing—engineering	128
3.8	Advance engineering	75
3.9	Design scheduling	49
3.10	Standard design engineering	542
3.13	Engineering liaison	350
	TOTAL	1,144

DOCUMENTING THE DESIGN—16%

3.11	Engineering changes	208
3.12	Engineering documentation	3,081
3.14	Manufacturing spec preparation	709
3.15	Manufacturing spec and system processing	498
3.16	Manufacturing spec documentation distribution	397
3.17	Manufacturing spec and documentation interp.	353
3.18	Change notice prior to manufacturing	190
	TOTAL	5,436

Table 11.1. Summary of Functions—Hours Per Month (continued)

SCHEDULING AND PLANNING FACTORY—5%

4.1	Manufacturing master scheduling	150
4.2	Manufacturing process planning	53
4.3	Parts routing	457
4.4	Standards applied to routed parts	1,058
4.5	Direct labor planning	74
	TOTAL	1,792

MATERIAL ACQUISITION AND CONTROL—15%

5.1	Inventory control	585
5.2	Vendor evaluation and selection	340
5.3	P.O. processing	425
5.4	P.O. monitoring and expediting	178
5.5	Vendor invoice processing	104
5.6	Material receiving	367
5.7	Receiving inspection	142
5.8	Stock control—raw	146
5.9	Stock control—components	2,499
5.10	Stock control—finished	292
5.11	Accounts payable	8
	TOTAL	5,086

FACTORY FLOOR LOADING AND RELEASE—4%

6.1	Factory floor loading and scheduling	309
6.3	Direct labor dispatching	923
	TOTAL	1,232

FACTORY FLOOR ACTIVITIES—28%

7.1	Work movement	3,020
7.2	In process inspection—machining	1,028
7.3	In process inspection—fabrication	168
7.4	Assembly inspection	359
7.5	Inspection documentation	65
7.6	Disposition N/C material	278
7.7	Shipping—domestic	17
7.8	Shipping—export	3
7.9	Timekeeping and labor reporting	837
7.10	Product order shipping	175
7.11	Expediting—late release	920
7.12	Expediting—spec modification	45
7.13	Expediting—misplaced materials	440
7.14	Expediting—misplaced documents	160
7.15	Expediting—scrapped	480
7.16	Expediting—miscellaneous	952
7.17	Expediting—inventory error	400
	TOTAL	9,347

Table 11.1. Summary of Functions—Hours Per Month (continued)

BILLING AND ACCOUNTING—1%

8.1	Order closeout	89
8.2	Billing and invoicing	8
8.3	Credit and collection	14
8.4	Cost accumulation and accounting	16
8.5	Cost analysis and control	49
2.1	Price policy administration	39
2.2	Gross margin analysis	51
2.3	Price book administration	73
	TOTAL	339

GENERAL SUPPORT ACTIVITIES—9%

9.1	General clerical	1,183
9.2	General factory supervision	744
9.3	Union relations	122
9.4	Technical training	112
9.5	Safety	58
9.6	Technical assistance	378
9.7	Employee relations	210
9.8	Factory maintenance	42
9.9	Machine repair	30
9.10	Office layout and expansion	26
9.11	Industrial engineering—miscellaneous studies	195
	TOTAL	3,100

PARTS, SERVICE AND WARRANTY—4%

10.1	Parts catalog preparation	984
10.2	Replacement parts sales	3
10.3	Service and warranty	250
10.4	Returned goods processing	124
	TOTAL	1,361

TOTAL HOURS/MONTH   33,957

Table 11.2. Monitoring, Expediting, and Scheduling Functions.

3.5	Order control and monitoring	494
7.11	Expediting due to late release	920
7.12	Expediting due to spec modification	45
7.13	Expediting due to misplaced materials	440
7.14	Expediting due to misplaced documents	160
7.15	Expediting due to scrapped materials	480
7.16	Expediting due to miscellaneous	952
7.17	Expediting due to inventory errors	400
	TOTAL	3,891

3.9	Design scheduling	49
4.1	Manufacturing master scheduling	150
6.1	Factory floor loading and scheduling	309
		508

Monitoring and expediting: 3,891   man-hours per month
Scheduling: 508
3,891/508 = 7.66

is equally important to identify those small functions which are being neglected, and to which *more* effort should be applied. Also, look for small functions that are important beyond their size because of their impact on other activities. For example, a very small amount of effort devoted to one function may create demands which cause other people to spend a large effort on another function.

Review, Refine Flow Diagrams

At this point, the whole O.F.A. team separates into the smaller improvement teams mentioned before. Each improvement team now refines and consolidates their operational and functional flow diagrams prepared during the information collection and analysis steps. If you have not already done so, calculate the O.F.A. ratios for the major functions, and display them on the functional flow diagram. Then trace the flow of the demands through the process. Concentrate especially on the alternate routes, and evaluate the O.F.A. ratios for each alternate route.

For example, Figure 11.1 shows a small portion of the total functional flow diagram for a typical equipment manufacturing business. It represents the first few steps in the order handling process. It is similar to Figure 10.11, but with the addition of O.F.A. ratios on the major functions.

A full function diagram, complete with demand volumes, functions hours, O.F.A. ratios, and alternate routes, is a great help in the subsequent evaluation and improvement identification steps, and in your final presentation of results to management. Prepare one that includes as many as you can of your organization's activities.

Caution. Remember, many of your functions will not fit neatly into a flow diagram, since they stand apart from the main work flow. Do not try to construct an artificial diagram for such functions, complete with a network of connecting lines. Show them as separate blocks, standing alone, as in fact they are.

Examine the Demands

Each improvement team now reviews the demands that drive the activities within their area of the O.F.A. program. Focus first on the

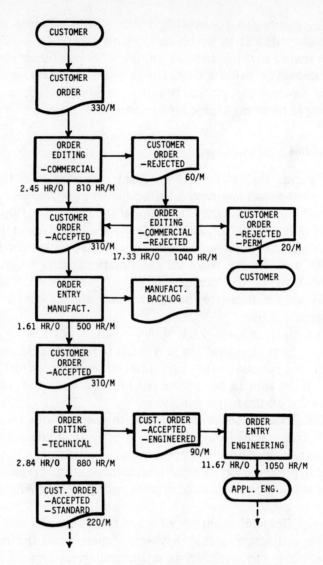

Figure 11.1

demands shown on your functional flow diagrams. Remember, however, that all demands may not appear on the diagrams. Look back over the list of demands you prepared at the start of the information collection process (Chapter 9), and the demands shown on the function summary sheets you prepared during the information analysis steps (Chapter 10).

Ask such questions as:

1. Is each major demand a valid, necessary part of doing business? Or is it an artificial, perhaps self-imposed demand? (Go back and review the material on demands in Chapter 5.)
2. Is it a secondary demand, with functional effort far beyond value received?
3. Can we reduce the volume of this demand and still maintain the same value of products and services to our customers?
4. What are the characteristics of this demand that influence and even determine the time and effort consumed by the associated functions?
5. Can we modify these demand characteristics and reduce the time and effort expended in satisfying the demand?
6. Is the demand internal or external? If internal, who in the organization should be working with us to reduce the impact? If external, who outside can work with us on this?

Look again at Figure 11.1. Look at the major demand(s) and ask the questions outlined above. Look into the head-end activities in your own organization. How do they stand up under the questions shown above?

Examine the Functions

Each improvement team now examines the functions within its scope. Review the flow diagrams, your original list of functions, and the functions shown on the function summary sheets. Continually ask such questions as:

1. Are there functions performed that are not really required by valid demands?
2. Are there any functions that are performed to meet reasonable demands, but which in turn place other invalid and unreasonable demands on downstream organizations?
3. Are there alternate routes through the functions? Should there be? Should there be more of them? Do the alternate routes begin early enough in the work flow? Too early?
4. Can we merge functions? That is, are there two or more functions, all in response to the same demand, that could be performed more productively if merged into one function?

5. Are any of the functions too dispersed, that is, spread throughout too many departments? Any too concentrated, which
should be divided among several departments?

Look at the functions in Figure 11.1. Think about the functions
in your own organization. How would you respond to these questions?

Examine the Operations

Most of your evaluations will focus on functions. However, in some
situations you will want to look at the detailed operations within a
function with questions such as:

1. Does this specific operation support a proper function? If
not, why is it performed?
2. Are there unnecessary operations, or missing ones that are
needed to accomplish valid functions?
3. Are the alternate routes through major operations satisfactory?
4. Can we merge operations, so that the same operations support
two or more functions?

An Example of Evaluation

Look once more at Figure 11.1. Let's evaluate this small portion of
work flow on the basis of the demand, functions and data shown
there. Here are some of the things we see.

First, the principal demand is the customer order. Approximately
330 orders are received each month, and they all pass through the
first function, order editing — commercial. Here people examine
each order, identify missing and erroneous information, and decide
whether or not the order is in shape to release through the in-house
processes. This function consumes 810 hours per month, or 2.45
hours per each order (O.F.A. ratio = 810/330 = 2.45).

Figure 11.1 also shows us that there are several different types of
customer orders, and after they all pass through this first function,
they divide, and each continues through a different alternate route.
As a result, some orders require substantially more effort than
others.

For instance, no errors are found on 270 orders, and they pass directly into the downstream activities. However, the remaining sixty orders contain errors, are rejected, and must go through an additional function, order editing — commercial — rejected. Here order analysts spend 1,040 hours per month contacting field salesmen and customers to correct the incomplete and erroneous information. The O.F.A. ratio tells us that each rejected order consumes an additional 17.33 hours as it passes through this function, for a total of 19.78 hours to this point (2.45 + 17.33 = 19.78).

Therefore, we can conclude that as it passes through the head-end editing process, an order that contains incomplete and inaccurate information requires more effort than a "clean" order by a factor of 8 : 1 (19.78/2.45 = 8.07)!

But that's not all. Figure 11.1 further shows that about 40 of the 60 rejected orders are corrected and returned to the main-line process. However, the remaining twenty orders are permanently rejected, and returned to the customers. That is, the order analysts conclude that these orders should not be accepted for many reasons. The order may call for products outside the normal product line, features not normally offered, unacceptable contract constraints, etc. Each such permanently rejected order consumes 19.78 hours before it returns to the customer, or 396 hours each month of totally unnecessary work (19.78 × 20 = 395.6)!

The great amount of time devoted to these two editing functions clearly suggests we have some problems here, along with real improvement opportunities. For example, if we could find ways to improve the completeness and accuracy of the customer orders, we very probably could reduce the first commercial editing by 50%, and save 405 man-hours each month (810 × 0.5 = 405).

Furthermore, these same improvements in the order accuracy could very well allow us to:

- Reduce by half the number of orders initially rejected but finally corrected (from 40 to 20) for a savings of 347 hours per month (17.33 × 20 = 346.6)
- Reduce the number of orders permanently rejected by 90% (from 20 to 2) for an additional savings of 356 hours (19.78 × 18 = 356).

In short, if we can significantly improve the completeness and accuracy of incoming customer orders, there is a potential savings of over 1,100 man-hours each month (405 + 347 + 356 = 1,108). That's a 60% reduction in order editing effort, and well worth going after (1,108/1,850 = 0.60).

Figure 11.1 shows us more. The surviving 310 orders now pass through the function order entry − manufacturing, where they are evaluated and placed in the manufacturing backlog. This consumes 500 hours a month, or 1.61 hours for each accepted order (500/310 = 1.61).

The orders then enter the next function, order editing − technical, where the order analysts decide whether the order can be satisfied with a standard product, or will require a specially engineered product. This function consumes 880 hours a month, or 2.84 hours per order (880/310 = 2.84).

In a typical month, the analysts find that 220 orders can be met with standard products, while 90 require some amount of engineering.

The engineered orders then go through the function order entry − engineering, where they are placed in the engineering schedule and backlog. This takes 1,050 hours each month, or 11.67 hours for each engineered order (1,050/90 = 11.67).

We said before that there were several different types of orders. In this little section of a functional flow diagram we have seen the following:

- Clean order for a standard product
  Effort required: 2.45 + 1.61 + 2.84 = 6.90 hours
- Clean order for engineered product
  Effort required: 2.45 + 1.61 + 2.84 + 11.67 = 18.57 hours
- Incomplete, inaccurate order for a standard product
  Effort required: 2.45 + 17.33 + 1.61 + 2.84 = 24.23 hours
- Incomplete, inaccurate order for an engineered product
  Effort required: 2.45 + 17.33 + 1.61 + 2.84 + 11.67 = 35.90 hours.

This shows us that in this head-end process alone, the effort to enter a customer order into the main-line process can easily vary by a ratio of over 5 : 1 (35.90/6.90 = 5.2). It clearly demonstrates that the nature of the demands (orders) greatly influences the effort consumed and the productivity of that effort. Chapters 15 and 18 present cases which further illustrate the concept of alternate routes.

An Important Point. The example shown in Figure 11.1 is for an equipment manufacturing business. However, a similar diagram could be drawn for the emergency receiving section of a hospital. Patients coming in are "edited:" minor child, requires parental approval; patient able to pay, adequate insurance; local resident; etc.

Some patients are permanently rejected (dead on arrival) or require special treatment available only at another hospital. Some patients can be treated in a "standard" manner in the emergency out-patient section. Others require "special" treatment and are sent to the main hospital for longer treatment and confinement.

Similarly, the head-end work flow in a very large commercial florist is not unlike Figure 11.1. Some orders are accepted, some are rejected, some cash, some credit. Some can be met with "standard" bouquets, while others require more elegant displays created by skilled artists.

Whatever type of organization you are analyzing, a functional flow diagram can serve as an excellent guide in your evaluation and improvement identification processes.

IMPROVEMENT IDENTIFICATION

The first part of this chapter described ways to evaluate the information we collected earlier, to make sense out of it, and see what it really means.

Evaluation is not enough. We must now identify ways to *improve* these activities. This improvement identification involves two major steps:

- Identification of the real problem
- Solution of the problem.

Problem Identification

This sounds easy. Surely we know what the problem is! But as you saw in Chapter 7, it is hard to separate the problem from the symptoms, especially in a modern, complex organization, where the cause may occur in one department, and the effects in other departments.

Fish Bone Diagrams

One of the best ways to separate the problem from its symptoms, and identify their relationships, is the cause and effect diagram,

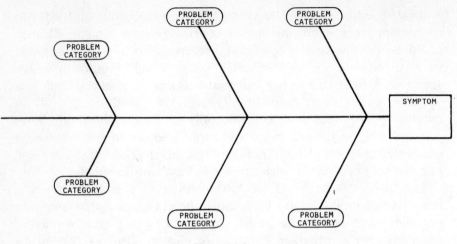

Figure 11.2

illustrated in Figure 11.2. It often is called a *fish bone diagram,* for reasons shown in Figure 11.3, and was first developed by Dr. Kaoru Ishikawa, professor at the University of Tokyo, as a part of his early work in the field of quality circles.

As indicated in Figure 11.2 and 11.3, difficulties in an organization often are symptoms of problems in one or more basic categories. On the manufacturing floor, for instance, these categories usually are

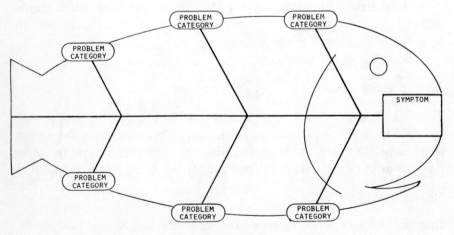

Figure 11.3

materials, methods, facilities, and people, so a fish bone diagram would look like Figure 11.4.

On the other hand, in office knowledge activities, the basic "material" is information, so the four factors are as shown in Figure 11.5:

- *Information.* Something is wrong with the information flowing into and through the process. Incomplete, inaccurate, insufficient, excessive.
- *Methods.* The "standard" method is inadequate. It might have been perfect when first introduced, but things have changed, new needs exist, and the process is no longer satisfactory.
- *Facilities.* Proper equipment and facilities are not available; inadequate maintenance; lack of "tools."
- *People.* Men and women in organization lack proper skills, attitudes, motivation.

When you use the fishbone diagram, you enter the symptom or effect in the box on the right. You then enter the possible problems or causes in the skeleton, placing each problem or cause along the proper bone, according to whether it is related to information, methods, facilities, or people.

Notice there are two empty bones in Figure 11.4 and 11.5. There may be major categories of problems or causes other than the four shown. For example, there may be causes related to company policies, to legal constraints, etc. There is no limit to the number of major bones that can be drawn on the diagram.

A Fish Bone Diagram Example

Our evaluation of the functional flow diagram in Figure 11.1 revealed symptoms of problems as well as improvement opportunities in these activities. Let's use a fish bone diagram to analyze this situation, and to identify some of the real problems that led to the difficulties mentioned there. Figure 11.6 shows this diagram.

First, enter the symptom on the diagram, in our case "excessive commercial editing" (a total of 1850 man-hours a month!).

Next, think of all the basic problems that might cause this symptom. Some people focus first on all the problems related to people, then facilities, then information, and finally method. Other people

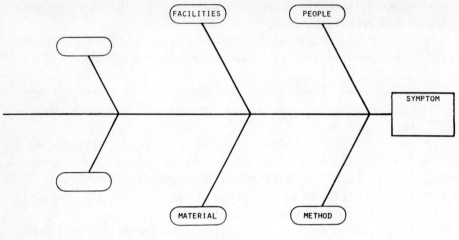

Figure 11.4

"brainstorm" all the problems, in no particular order, and enter them on the proper bone as they think of them. Only a few problems are shown on Figure 11.6.

People problems

- We are all controlled by habit. "We always have done it this way. Why change?"

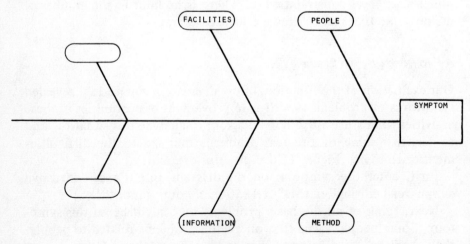

Figure 11.5

- "We don't trust salesmen. They're a slippery bunch. We always check everything they do twice to make sure."

Method problems

- Customer orders come in many different types of formats. Each customer has his own order form. This makes it very difficult to edit the commercial details.
- The field salesmen do not use the special order data sheets to summarize the order details. They say the reason for this is that. . . .
- The order data sheets are obsolete and confusing.

Information problems

- Customer orders contain incomplete and inaccurate information, hence require a considerable amount of commercial order editing.

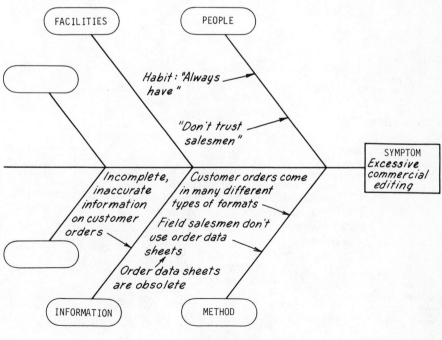

Figure 11.6

Facilities problems. None are apparent.

At this point, we might pursue any of these basic problems. Whichever we select, we probably will find that it is not really a basic problem, only a symptom of another, more remote problem. To illustrate this, let's look at the problem shown on Figure 11.6, "incomplete, inaccurate information on customer orders," and draw another fish bone diagram, Figure 11.7.

First, we enter the "problem" — in this case recognized as a symptom — into the symptom box. Then we think of problems which may contribute and cause this symptom. A few are shown in Figure 11.7.

People problems

- Salesmen understand neither how orders are produced nor the need for timely information on these orders.

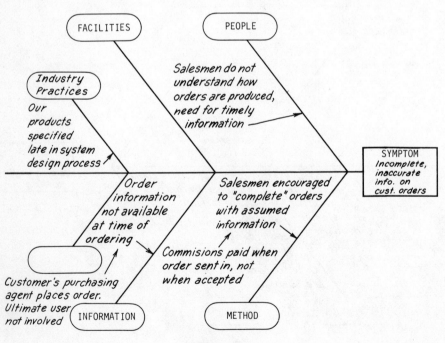

Figure 11.7

Methods problems

- The current method of order entry encourages field salesmen to send in orders as fast as possible, even if they "complete" an order with assumed information, which must be discovered and corrected during the commercial editing process. The reason for this is that. . . .
- Sales commissions are paid on the basis of the date the order is submitted from the field sales office, not the date the order is *accepted* and *entered* into the business.

Information problems

- Much of the order information is not available at the time of ordering, hence cannot be entered into the customer order data sheet, because. . . .
- Customer's purchasing agent gives the order to our field salesman. The actual user does not get involved in this contact, even though he often knows some of the missing information.

Industry practices

- The equipment made by this company is used by customers as a part of a complex system, along with other, larger, more expensive equipment. Consulting engineers who design these systems specify this other equipment first, and then specify our company's equipment much later. As a result, many of the orders have incomplete or assumed information, later found to be wrong through the commercial editing process.

Notice four things about the diagrams in Figures 11.6 and 11.7. First, you can cascade *between* fish bone diagrams. For example, "incomplete, inaccurate information on customer orders," a problem in Figure 11.6, becomes the symptom on Figure 11.7.

Second, you can cascade *within* a single diagram. In Figure 11.6, we see that "excessive commercial editing" is caused in part by field salesmen who do not use the order data sheets. This, in turn, is caused by obsolete data sheets. In some cases, it is best to show these cascading relationships between diagrams, and sometimes within.

Third, do not hesitate to add new categories as appropriate to your situation, such as industry practices in Figure 11.7.

Fourth, it is not always obvious on which bone you should place a problem. In Figure 11.6, "customer orders come in many different types of formats" can be on the method problems bone, as shown, or on the information problems bone instead. The important thing is to get all significant problems on the diagram, and to illustrate their cause-and-effect relationships.

Problem Solution

Once the improvement teams have identified the real problems, they then identify the solutions.

This is not easy. In office, knowledge activities, these productivity problems are complex. Solutions are seldom obvious; we can easily be deflected from the optimum answer, and the problem remains unsolved. This situation can be avoided by following a solution plan, a road map to guide us through this process to a satisfactory solution. Such a plan is illustrated in Figure 11.8.

It is important to start the solution process with the right question. Too often a person will propose a solution this way: "Why can't we solve this problem by . . . ?"

This is wrong. It is much better to start the solution process with a positive question: "In what way can we solve this problem?" This establishes a constructive environment, and greatly increases the chances of successful solution.

Don't be satisfied with just one proposed solution. Gather as many as possible before you continue the process. The more proposed solutions you can identify, the greater the chances that one of them will be a real winner.

Once you have identified a number of potential solutions, take each one through the process shown in Figure 11.8. In some cases you will hit an immediate "yes" answer. Fine. However, in many other cases you will have a "yes and no" response. Then you must stratify the problem, divide it into several smaller ones, which you may be able to solve individually.

You may hit a "no" answer to your proposed solution. Don't be put off and deflected. Often this results from constraints, many

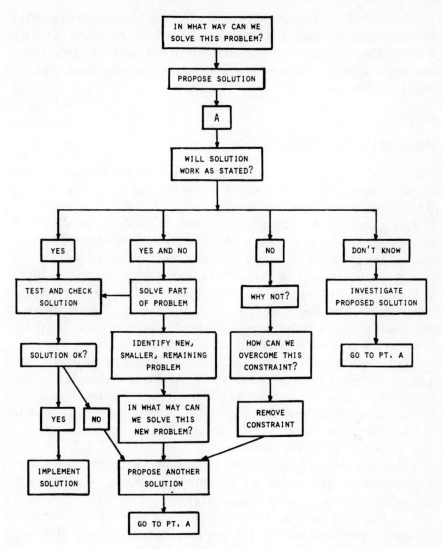

Figure 11.8

self-imposed. Once this fact is recognized, you can propose another solution that removes or bypasses a constraint.

In some cases, you simply will not know if the suggested solution is feasible. Investigate further, and then start the solution process again.

Caution. Do not be satisfied with the first proposed solution that safely passes through the labyrinth. Feed *all* proposed solutions through the process. Retain those that survive, and evaluate them on the basis of your judgment, or traditional economic measures, and select the one you prefer.

IMPROVEMENT DOCUMENTATION

The preceding sections described the evaluation and the improvement identification processes. But this is not all that is needed. We must document these recommendations.

Too often a productivity improvement report consists of one section that contains a great amount of background data and observations, and another section containing the recommended improvements and changes. This may seem reasonable, but with this format it is next to impossible to identify the relationships between the observations and the resulting recommendations. Senior managers are confused, and often reject excellent recommendations because they cannot recognize these important relationships.

Your improvement teams can avoid this by using the observation and recommendation summary sheet, shown in Figure 11.9. Both quantitative data and qualitative observations are entered on the left of the page, describing the conditions as they now exist, and the needs for improvement. The recommended improvements and changes are listed on the right side.

This disciplined approach accomplishes two important things. First, it forces the improvement team members to sharpen their thinking, to make sure that their recommendations are in fact supported by and in response to valid observations. Second, it allows the senior managers and others who receive the report to more effectively evaluate it.

Figure 11.9 contains observations based on the cause-and-effect analysis shown in Figures 11.6 and 11.7. Notice that only selected data and observations are shown in Figure 11.9 — just those needed to support the associated recommendations. Subsequent sheets would document other observations and recommendations.

OBSERVATIONS	RECOMMENDATIONS
EXCESSIVE TIME DEVOTED TO EDITING COMMERCIAL INFORMATION ON CUSTOMER ORDERS. IN TYPICAL MONTH, ALL 330 ORDERS PASS THROUGH INITIAL FUNCTION, ORDER EDITING—COMMERCIAL, CONSUMING 810 MAN-HOURS PER MONTH.	1. ESTABLISH A TIME-PHASED PROCESS FOR ACCUMULATING AND ENTERING INFORMATION ON ORDERS SO THAT THE SEQUENCE OF RECEIPT OF ORDER INFORMATION IS CONSISTENT WITH THE TIMING AND SEQUENCE OF USE OF THIS SAME INFORMATION IN THE INTERNAL PROCESSING OF ORDER.
SIXTY OUT OF THESE 330 ORDERS ARE REJECTED BY THIS INITIAL EDIT, AND REQUIRE FURTHER EDITING AND FOLLOWUP WITH FIELD SALES AND CUSTOMERS, FOR ANOTHER 1,040 HRS/MONTH, FOR TOTAL OF 1,850 HOURS. ABOUT 20 OF THESE 60 FAIL THIS SECOND EDIT, AND ARE PERMANENTLY REJECTED AND RETURNED TO CUSTOMERS.	2. EXTEND THE MASTER SCHEDULE OF THE BUSINESS TO INCLUDE THE PREPARATION OF THE PROPOSAL AND THE RECEIPT OF THE CUSTOMER ORDER, BASED ON STANDARD LEAD TIMES FOR PROCESSING THE ORDERS THROUGH ALL STEPS OF THE BUSINESS. THESE LEAD TIMES SHOULD IN TURN BE BASED ON THE TIME-PHASED PROCESS MENTIONED IN RECOMMENDATION NO. 1, ABOVE.
THERE ARE SEVERAL REASONS FOR THIS EXCESSIVE EDITING. MAJOR ONE IS THAT COMMERCIAL DATA ON INCOMING CUSTOMER ORDERS ARE INCOMPLETE AND INACCURATE. THIS IN TURN OCCURS BECAUSE: (1) OUR PRODUCTS ARE INTEGRATED INTO COMPLEX ELECTRICAL-MECHANICAL SYSTEM, AND TRADITIONALLY ARE SPECIFIED LATE IN THE CUSTOMERS DESIGN PROCESS. (2) ULTIMATE USER OF OUR EQUIPMENT IN CUSTOMER ORGANIZATION (SYSTEM ENGINEER) NOT INVOLVED IN PLACING ORDER. CUSTOMER'S PURCASING STAFF CANNOT SUPPLY NEC-ESSARY INFORMATION. (3) OUR FIELD SALESMEN DO NOT UNDERSTAND HOW THE COMMERCIAL INFORMATION IS USED INTERNALLY IN PROCESSING ORDERS, HENCE CANNOT EXPLAIN OUR INFORMATION NEEDS TO CUSTOMERS.	3. TRAIN ALL FIELD SALESMEN IN THE INTERNAL ORDER HANDLING PROCESS SO THEY WILL BE EQUIPPED TO EXPLAIN THE ORDER INFORMATION NEEDS TO OUR CUSTOMERS AND ENCOURAGE THEIR ADHERENCE TO THE RELATED SCHEDULES FOR INFORMATION SUBMIS-SION.
	4. HAVE FIELD SALESMEN DEMONSTRATE TO CUSTOMERS THE NEED FOR THEIR SYSTEM ENGINEERS TO PARTICIPATE IN PLACING ORDERS TO ENSURE THAT ACCURATE AND TIMELY INFORMATION IS FURNISHED.

THE BUMBARGER GROUP / Atlanta

Figure 11.9

In a series of working sessions, the entire O.F.A. team reviews all sheets, and combines and extends as appropriate. The draft sheets are then typed in the final form shown in Figure 11.9.

SUMMARY

At the start of the evaluation process, the entire O.F.A. team reviews all key observations, and examines all work flow functions. They then divide into several smaller improvement teams, each continuing the evaluation in an assigned area of the organization's activities.

With evaluation complete, the members turn to improvement identification, which is divided into two parts: problem identification and problem solution.

One of the best tools for problem identification is the cause-and-effect or fish bone diagram. Problem solution should use a process like that illustrated in Figure 11.8.

Documentation is the final step in the evaluation and improvement identification process. Conclusion and recommendation summary sheets ensure that all recommendations are based on valid conclusions, not preconceived notions.

Chapter 12
Implementation Planning and Recommendation

The preceding chapter described how to evaluate the information you have collected, and identify potential improvements in your organization's activities based on these evaluations.

This chapter describes the next step: how to define specific improvement projects, plan their implementation, and report their conclusions to the senior managers.

DEFINITION OF IMPROVEMENT PROJECTS

Earlier, you documented your recommendations on observation and recommendation summary sheets (Figure 11.9) so as to ensure a close correlation with their supporting observations. Senior managers always are interested in seeing these sheets, and you will include them in your final report.

However, more is needed. Look again at the recommendations shown on the right side of Figure 11.9. Good though they may be, they are only a beginning. Notice how each begins with an action word: "establish," "extend," "train," "have." That is, they say *what* should be done, but nothing about *how* it should be done. Therefore, as the next step, you must clearly define specific projects through which you will *implement* these improvements.

Improvement Project Sheet

There are many ways to do this. One is the improvement project sheet, the front side of which is illustrated in Figure 12.1, and the reverse in Figure 12.2. The improvement team prepares one of these sheets for each of their improvement projects, showing the specific

179

THE
BUMBARGER
GROUP

IMPROVEMENT PROJECT SUMMARY SHEET

SPECIFIC RECOMMENDATION: Establish time-phased process for accumulating and
entering information on orders so sequence of receipt of order information is consistent with timing and sequence of use of same information in
internal processing order. Currently, some information received first is
not used until late in design/manufacturing cycle. Example: shipping
destinations and carriers. Other information received later is needed
early in design/manufacturing cycle. Example: Many items of design information. When this information is missing on incoming order, time is consumed in order editing. When this information is received and entered
late into process, extra handling, expediting and processing effort is consumed.

ANTICIPATED BENEFITS: Currently, 810 hrs/month spent editing all incoming
orders, 1040 hrs editing orders with missing or incomplete commercial
information, 880 hrs editing technical features, 1700 hrs on special
processing when information is entered into process at later time. This
totals at least 4430 hrs. Implementation of this recommendation, along
with recommendations 2, 3, 4, 7, and 14, will reduce this at least 60%,
or 2658 hrs/month. Furthermore, we anticipate minimum reduction of two
weeks in design/manufacturing cycle time for each order.

AREAS OF IMPACT (FUNCTIONS, ORGANIZATIONS): Order editing, entry, follow-up,
expediting, advance engineering, production engineering, production planning and control. Organizations: field sales, inside sales, application
and design engineering.

Figure 12.1

recommendations, anticipated benefits, areas of impact, required
implementation actions, and significant interfaces. Since frequently
there are overlaps between improvement teams, two or more teams
may join forces to define and prepare the sheet for a project in which
they share an interest and responsibility.

IMPLEMENTING ACTIONS - SCHEDULE, DESCRIPTION AND RESPONSIBILTIES

1.   Identify principal product modules used in scheduling material

     acquisition and factory production releases, for each major

     type of product.

     Resp.: Manufacturing Planning   Completion Date:

2.   Identify lead times before order shipping date when design

     information must be released from engineering to manufacturing

     planning for these modules.

     Resp.: Manufacturing Planning   Completion Date:

3.   Determine engineering cycle times required to prepare this

     design information.

     Resp.: Engineering Administration   Completion Date:

4.   On the basis of the above information, determine and document

     the lead times before order shipping date when information must

     must be received from customer/field sales.

     Resp.: Inside Sales   Completion Date:

5.   Design and produce new order data sheet forms which show

     required lead times for all information. Establish new

     procedures and instructions for their use.

     Resp.: Inside Sales   Completion Date:

INTERFACES: Check with overseas subsidiaries that sometimes ship directly to

our customers and factor in their leads when appropriate.

_____

_____

_____

_____

Figure 12.2

Figures 12.1 and 12.2 describe a project for implementing the first recommendation shown on the observation and recommendation sheet in Figure 11.9. Notice the following:

Specific Recommendation. This expands on the recommendation shown in Figure 11.9 and gives more background information on the problems leading to this solution.

Anticipated Benefits. In a similar manner, this section extends the benefits suggested in Figure 11.9. It mentions potential savings associated with 1,700 hours per month devoted to special processing due to incomplete and inaccurate information on incoming orders. These 1,700 hours and the related recommendations 7 and 14 are associated with other parts of the business, hence are documented on other summary sheets not shown here.

Areas of Impact. Several functions and related organizations are listed here. Do not try to list every possible one, since this section is used to indicate a general range of impact.

Implementing Actions. As shown in Figure 12.2, this is an outline of the major work tasks in this implementation project. The organization the improvement team feels should be responsible for each task is shown. The completion date will not be entered until after the recommendations have been reviewed by senior managers.

Interfaces. Often an implementation project will relate to activities in another part of the business. If these interfaces are not obvious, they should be described here so they will not be missed during the project.

IMPROVEMENT PROJECT PLANNING

The typical O.F.A. program results in approximately 30–100 improvement projects, involving many different areas of the organization. Clearly, they cannot, nor should be implemented at the same time. We need to do three things:

1. Assign a priority to each project
2. Identify which departments within the total organization will be impacted by the project
3. Establish a time-phase plan for all implementation projects, based on the first two factors above.

Project Priorities

Figure 12.3 shows a project priority sheet on which each improvement team lists and ranks its implementation projects. Later, the

PROJECT PRIORITY SHEET

DESCRIPTION OF PROJECT	BENEFIT	URGENCY	EASE	TOTAL

Figure 12.3

entire O.F.A. team consolidates and reviews the priorities of all projects.

With this sheet, each implementation project is evaluated on the basis of three factors: potential benefits, urgency, and ease of implementation. A typical evaluation scale is shown in Table 12.1.

For example, consider three improvement implementation projects with the following evaluations:

Project A. New automated material storage and retrieval system for warehouse:

- Would help only a little to implement this improvement, since this is not a high-volume warehouse (benefit rating = 1)
- Do not need solution right now, since we plan to move warehouse activities to new site about one year from now (urgency rating = 1)
- Very difficult to do, would require considerable amount of system design work, very large outside investment (ease rating = 1)

Total priority evaluation for Project A = 3 points.

Project B. New system for receiving and processing customer service requests:

- Would be a very great help, with major improvements in the time spent on receiving requests, scheduling and dispatching service crews, and in customer satisfaction (benefit rating = 4)
- Need implementation and solution as soon as possible; have had this problem for years; could have used a good solution months ago (urgency rating = 4)
- Tough to do (ease rating = 2)

Total priority evaluation for Project B = 10 points.

Project C. New work request system for office maintenance department:

- Would help a fair amount; roughly 20% of time of maintenance staff now wasted due to false starts resulting from poor work orders; four lost-time accidents occurred in office areas last year

due to inadequate maintenance, due in turn to "lost" maintenance requests (benefit rating = 2)
- Could use solution quite soon; office maintenance crew will be working full-time on major renovations for next three weeks; could use solution immediately after that (urgency rating = 3)
- Could accomplish solution in less than one week; need to design new work request form, print new forms, distribute instructions (ease rating = 4)

Total priority evaluation for Project C = 9 points.

Which of these significantly different improvement projects should be done first? Clearly, we would lean towards projects B and C. We probably should do project C first, even though it has a smaller

Table 12.1. Project Priority Ratings.

PRIORITY FACTOR	PRIORITY DESCRIPTION	PRIORITY POINTS
Potential benefits	Would help only a little to solve this problem, and would bring only uncertain benefits	1
	Would help a fair amount to solve this problem	2
	Would help a lot	3
	Would be a very great help to solve this problem, with major improvements in productivity, effort, cycle times	4
Urgency of implementation	No rush—really don't need solution very soon	1
	Could use solution within next few months	2
	Could use solution quite soon	3
	Need solution as soon as possible, yesterday would have been better	4
Ease of implementation	Very difficult to implement solution; probably would need outside help, large investment	1
	Tough to do	2
	Probably could accomplish solution in few weeks	3
	Very easy, a snap, piece of cake	4

overall priority rating than B, because the ease of implementation rating for project C is significantly larger than for project B. That is, we can almost immediately implement C, and begin to harvest the benefits, even though they may be smaller than the benefits of B.

Caution. Don't make a number exercise out of this. Use the ratings as only a first guide. Use your judgment in the final analysis.

Caution. The priority descriptions shown in Table 12.1 are very general. In practice, develop your own, more precise descriptions. For example, quantify the potential benefits and the ease of implementation. Develop payback ratios between benefits and costs of implementation, as described in the next chapter.

Improvement Project Impact

The implementation plan for your O.F.A. program not only must recognize the relative priorities of the individual improvement projects, but also must recognize the impact these same projects will have on the different departments and groups within your organization.

These relationships are presented on the improvement impact summary sheet, Figure 12.4. This sheet was prepared by an improvement team in an equipment manufacturing and distribution business, and focuses on product engineering activities.

Improvement implementation projects are listed down the left side of the sheet. The next column shows the organization responsible for coordinating each project. The total anticipated improvement is shown for each project, measured in internal man-hours per month, external costs per month, and cycle time. This total improvement then is divided among the departments. For the projects shown in Figure 12.4, the improvement team members anticipated only improvements in internal man-hours. No further savings were expected in external costs nor cycle times.

For example, they expected that the first project would result in total savings in internal effort of 162 man-hours per month, 90 of which would occur in the specification engineering organization, and the remaining 72 in engineering services. In projects 6 and 8, they

IMPROVEMENT IMPACT SUMMARY SHEET
ACTIVITIES: PRODUCT ENGINEERING

OPERATION FUNCTION ANALYSIS

NO.	IMPROVEMENT IMPLEMENTATION PROJECT DESCRIPTION	COORDINATING RESPONSIBILITY	PLANNED IMPLEMENTATION DATE	TOTAL ANTICIPATED IMPROVEMENT MAN HOURS	CYCLE TIME $	Spec. Eng'g MAN HOURS	CYCLE TIME $	Spec. Drftg. MAN HOURS	CYCLE TIME $	Eng. Services MAN HOURS	CYCLE TIME $	Purchasing MAN HOURS	CYCLE TIME $	MAN HOURS $	CYCLE TIME $	REMARKS
1	Combine DTR-Job Ref Dwg & Microfilm Req.	Spec. Eng'g		162		90				72						
2	Eliminate req't for A-C dwgs on P.O.'s	Purch		62						62						
3	Revise computer data base & program to generate "0102" list	Mngnt Syst.		62*						30*		32				
4	Incr. LV cert'd jobs & elim. approvals	Field Sales		298		69		219		10						
5	Incr. HV cert'd jobs & reduce appr's 50%	Field Sales		332		72		249		11						
6	Increase use of computer W/D on HV	Spec. Eng'g		77				83		(6)						
7	Up-date cat. file and complete part	Spec. Drftg.		137		59		78								
8	Transfer P.O. typing from Spec. Eng'g to Purchasing and revise routing	Purch.		68*		81		27*				(40)				Project No. 8 can be implemented only by absorbing present P.O. typing into Purchasing Department. Suggestions are in process to do this with no added personnel. If this is possible, then (40) hrs shown here would be zero.
	TOTAL POTENTIAL IMPROVEMENTS			1171		371		629*		179*		(8)				

* 27 hours in #3 and #8 are identical so if both are implemented, count only once in totals.

THE BUMBARGER GROUP / Atlanta

Figure 12.4

expected the effort to increase in purchasing and engineering services from their changes. However, this would be more than offset by reductions in effort in other organizations. No planned completion dates were shown in Figure 12.4 because this sheet was prepared before the projects were reviewed with senior managers and the final implementation schedule established.

Figure 12.5 shows an improvement impact summary sheet for the projects first identified on the observation and recommendation summary sheet in Figure 11.9. In this case, four projects have been grouped together, since the savings shown in Figure 12.5 can be gained only if all four projects are completed. The sheet indicates that the coordinating responsibility should be assigned to inside sales. As before, no implementation date is shown because the firm schedule has not been established.

Figure 12.5 shows that in our order processing case, we expect savings in all three categories: internal effort; external costs (largely communication expenses associated with chasing missing information on customer orders); and cycle time.

At this point in your O.F.A. program, each improvement team should prepare a draft set of improvement impact summary sheets listing their projects. Some projects may overlap two or more improvement teams, so be ready to work together as you prepare your draft sheets. When this is done, the entire O.F.A. team reviews and consolidates this information and prepares a final set of improvement impact summary sheets.

Phased Implementation Plan

Once the priorities have been established for each implementation project, and the improvement impact summary sheets have been completed, then prepare a time-phased implementation plan. Later, after review and modification by the senior managers, this plan becomes the implementation schedule.

The implementation of knowledge work improvements is very different from the implementation of improvements in direct labor and material. For example, an engineer can redesign the product, reduce the direct labor content, and immediately achieve a labor

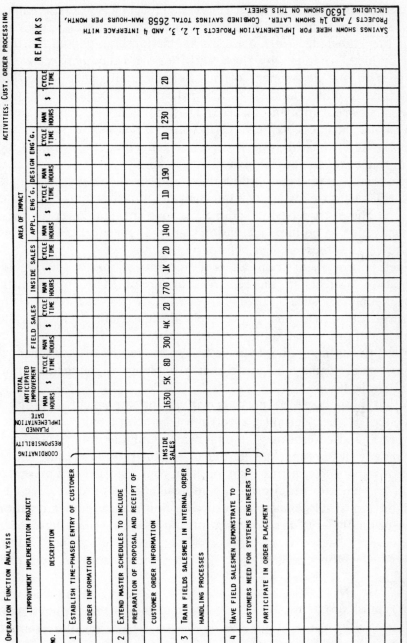

Figure 12.5

savings. Similarly, a purchasing buyer can locate a lower cost vendor for material, and immediately achieve a material savings.

In the knowledge work areas, these relationships seldom are that well defined. That is why these activities are called *indirect* work. Changes in one department often result in improvements in other departments. Potential savings in effort, external expense, and cycle times may occur in many places in these other areas. Furthermore, in a smaller business, savings may involve "fractions" of people, half a person here, two-thirds over there, one and a quarter persons in the next group, as is the case shown in Figure 12.4.

Too many traditional productivity improvement programs miss their mark because managers implement the improvements but fail to capture these dispersed fractional savings in manpower. A well thought out phased implementation plan will prevent this and enable you to capture these savings before they vanish.

Each improvement team enters the priority rating for their implementation projects in the remarks column of their improvement impact summary sheets. Examine your list of projects, evaluate the priority codes, and the impact relationships, and decide on the sequence of implementation for these projects.

Next, the entire O.F.A. team combines the results of the individual improvement teams, and establishes a sequence of implementation for all projects.

In a typical case, the projects will *not* be implemented in direct sequence. Rather, certain projects must be completed before others can start, and several may be underway simultaneously. Therefore, you may wish to prepare a Gantt chart to illustrate these time-phased relationships, and use this chart both in your management presentations, and later for monitoring the implementation process. (See any text on industrial engineering or production planning for a detailed description of Gantt chart preparation and use.)

REPORTS TO MANAGEMENT

Written Report

In a typical program, the O.F.A. team members prepare a formal, written report, usually divided into two parts: background and results.

The background section describes the O.F.A. process, the program objectives, scope, team participation and general schedule.

The results section typically contains the following material:

- A summary of functions, showing the man-hours of effort devoted to each function, as illustrated in Table 11.1
- A functional flow chart showing the relationships of these activities (a small piece is shown in Figure 11.1)
- Observation and recommendation summary sheets (Figure 11.9)
- Improvement project summary sheets (Figure 12.1)
- Improvement impact summary sheets (Figure 12.4)
- A Gantt chart or similar diagram showing the time-phased sequence of project implementation
- Definition of functions, function summary sheets (Figure 10.8), and O.F.A. ratio summary sheets (Figure 10.9).

Oral Report

Your oral report to your senior managers should hit only the highlights of the total written report. Briefly review the summary of functions (Table 11.1) to give them an overview of the major activities of their business, and the relative effort assigned to each major function. Show them the functional flow diagram so they can better envision the relationships between these functions. Devote most of your oral report to a discussion of the major observations and recommendation sheets (Figure 11.9). Finish with a brief review of the major improvement project summary sheets (Figure 12.1), the improvement impact summary sheets (Figure 12.4), and the proposed time-phased sequence of implementation.

At the completion of the oral report, urge your senior managers to thoroughly read all aspects of your written report, and be ready for additional working sessions as the first step in the improvement implementation process, described in Chapter 13.

Sell Your Recommendations

It is not enough to prepare and present your reports to your senior managers, no matter how excellent these reports may be.

In Chapter 3, we learned that improvement requires change, and that change requires creativity. Change also requires salesmanship. In fact, the final success of your O.F.A. program will depend on your ability to sell your recommendations, first to your senior managers, and later to your colleagues during the improvement implementation process.

There are many ways to do this. Figure 12.6 illustrates six major ways to seek change.* Half of Figure 12.6 presents safe approaches, and half risky ones. In general, the safe methods are less effective than the risky ones. It is important to understand these so you will know which to use and which to avoid. This is especially important in your presentations to senior managers, because their reaction to change will be reflected throughout the entire organization.

The least effective positive way to change an organization – but very safe – is shown at the top of the diagram. Using it, you quietly suggest general changes and try to push through the "molasses wall" of apathy that often exists in an organization. Usually you get stuck in the molasses. Nothing happens. No one is affected one way or the other. This is the usual end to many productivity improvement programs.

Moving around the diagram counterclockwise, we find the lowest risk, positive approach to selling change. You inquire, ask leading questions, and hope that these questions will get people in the organization to think about the need for and benefits obtained from the change. Usually you will get a flood of glittering, pleasant explanations in response to your questions – and sometimes a small amount of constructive change.

The third approach is generally the most difficult to sell, but sometimes can be the most effective safe method. Armed with the facts, you attempt to pin down the people in are area, hoping they then will change. If the people are very cooperative, this approach sometimes works, since their evasion will be slight.

If they only give the *appearance* of cooperation, and are in fact uncooperative – watch out! Since their evasion does not occur immediately, the process *appears* to work. However, as soon as you

---

*I am indebted to an unknown benefactor who sketched a similar diagram on a placemat in the restaurant of the Red Carpet Inn, Milwaukee, Wisconsin, several years ago, and left it behind for me to see!

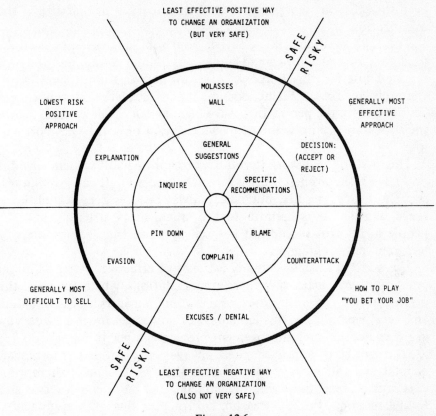

Figure 12.6

are out of sight, the strong evasion starts in full force, and little permanent change and improvement occurs. This happens often with traditional improvement programs forced on an organization from the outside.

Continuing around counterclockwise to the risky side of the diagram, the least effective negative way to change an organization is shown at the bottom of the diagram. Armed with some facts, you can complain to people about their activities, and they will respond with excuses and denials.

One side or the other will eventually give in. If they run out of excuses, you'll get your way — until you leave; then things will return to normal. If they do *not* run out of excuses, and you keep complaining, you will establish your reputation as a complainer, and even though you are right, you will be thrown out of that area of the organization.

The fifth method, the "you bet your job" approach, typically is used by external auditors and some consultants. Sometimes they are retained just for this purpose. After an investigation, they identify the problem, fix the blame, document and circulate their report, and get out before the people they have blamed can counterattack. Since their jobs are secure with their own external firm, they have little to lose.

This method can work if you have unimpeachable evidence, and if you have been given authority for such a crusade. It can give impressive short-range results, but nearly always causes deep-seated, long-range damage. It is harmful to the organization structure and the people in it. This should not be used in a constructive productivity improvement program.

The sixth approach generally is the most effective. After an initial evaluation, you make specific recommendations, which people in the organization — in your case, your senior managers — can examine and accept or reject. This encourages them to get involved with you in the evaluation and improvement process in a positive manner.

With this sixth approach, there always is the risk that your recommendations will be rejected — but if they are accepted, there is an excellent chance they will be implemented in a constructive and lasting manner. For this reason, O.F.A. uses this sixth approach to the greatest degree possible.

SUMMARY

The implementation planning and recommendation process described in this chapter involves three main steps:

Define specific implementation projects. In this step, we review the observation and recommendation sheets prepared earlier, identify specific projects to implement these recommendations, and document these projects on improvement project summary sheets.

Implementation project planning. All improvement projects cannot, and should not, occur at the same time. Therefore we assign a priority to each project, examine the impact the projects will have on all departments of the organization, and establish a time-phased implementation plan.

Reports to management. Both oral and written reports are presented by the O.F.A. team to their senior managers. The overall success of your O.F.A. program will depend on your ability to sell your recommendations both to your senior managers and your colleagues.

Now, let's move on to the last step in the O.F.A. process, improvement implementation.

Chapter 13
Improvement Implementation

We have completed Phase 1 (senior management introduction and planning) and Phase 2 (middle management analysis and recommendation). The O.F.A. team has documented its final recommendations and presented them to senior management. We are now ready to move into the final Phase 3 (improvement implementation).

Confirm Priorities and Implementation Plan

In their oral report, the O.F.A. team members touched only on the major recommendations. The senior managers now must study the report in detail, and evaluate each specific recommendation. It is typical for the president or division general manager to request a written response from each subordinate senior manager on every recommendation in the report. As the responses are received, a score sheet is prepared showing each senior manager's evaluation of the specific items.

In a group session, the senior managers and O.F.A. team members review the score sheets and prepare a final version of their phased implementation plan.

Caution. Do not be surprised if senior managers reject some team recommendations. After all, it is much better to have the team members stretch their minds and develop really bold, even audacious solutions to major problems — and have some rejected by senior managers — than for team members to retain their old habits and biases, and develop modest solutions to insignificant problems — and have none rejected.

Because an O.F.A. program often deals with major changes in organizational processes and structures on which senior managers may have widely divergent views, the C.E.O. or general manager may have to make the final, reconciling decision.

Recommend Responsibilities for Implementation

The O.F.A. team members then:

- Group related projects
- Identify task forces for implementing these projects
- Recommend a senior manager to monitor, and a chairperson and assistant chairperson to direct each task force. These latter two need not be members of the O.F.A. Team. However, they should be in the line management of the affected area.

The package of projects shown in Figure 13.1 involves product engineering activities in an equipment manufacturing and distribution business. The monitoring senior manager and the two people assigned to lead the task force are shown at the head of the sheet. Project numbers and descriptions are shown in the body of the page, along with a two-level priority evaluation. These implementation assignment sheets should be a principal tool in planning and monitoring the improvements.

Implement the Improvements

Now the O.F.A. process shifts from the program mode to the line management mode. That is, the president or general manager disbands the O.F.A. team, and confirms the responsibilities for each task force shown on the implementation assignment sheets.

These assignments become an integral part of the day-by-day work. Each participant's work goals and objectives are extended to include his work on the task force, and he should be evaluated on this basis.

Each senior manager should monitor the progress of his task force against set schedules, and report this progress to the president or division general manager as part of his regular management reports.

Measure the Results

Many of the most valuable benefits derived from an O.F.A. program may be intangible, such as improvements in customer satisfaction,

OPERATION FUNCTION ANALYSIS PROGRAM

IMPLEMENTATION ASSIGNMENT SHEET

TASK FORCE: Product Engineering Documentation

RESP. SR. MGR.: T. R. Banderson

CHAIRMAN: Emily Walker   ASSIST. CHAIRMAN: Bill Cranker

PRIORITY		DESCRIPTION OF IMPLEMENTATION PROJECT
High	(27)	Establish a new Divisional Engineering Standards Department.
	(28)	Select and train person located at Plant No. 2 to handle both Engineering Standards and Data Control activities.
	(29)	Introduce new paperwork handling system that will route E.R.N. directly through Plant No. 2 Engineering Standards Department, bypassing Main Plant.
	(30)	Conduct classes in correct preparation on new E.R.N. documents.
	(37)	Secure engineering records vault to ensure that only authorized personnel enter this area.
	(93)	Expand Order Completion Forms to include descriptions of repetitive items not now listed.
	(94)	Revise and expand requisitions generated by Design Engineering Department so same record can be used to request necessary information from Purchasing Department, which can in turn request it from vendor.
	(97)	Define and document higher quality standards for Engineering documents.
Low	(14)	Develop level by level indented bills of materials for all new product lines.
	(35)	Develop new storage approaches for all existing drawings.
	(36)	Conduct thorough studies of personnel and machine requirements for future drawing production.

Figure 13.1

increased employee commitment to company goals and objectives, reduction in order processing cycle times, etc.

Other improvements will be very tangible, with measurable savings in both internal effort and external expenses. Managers may wish to measure these tangible benefits as part of their evaluation of the O.F.A. program. This can be easily done, based on two indicators.

Payback Ratio

This is the ratio of the continuing annual savings to the one-time investment in the program:

$$\text{Payback ratio} = \frac{\text{Continuing annual savings}}{\text{One-time investment}}$$

At the beginning of the program, senior managers may suggest a goal to the O.F.A. team members, say a payback ratio of 3 : 1. This ratio can be calculated at the end of Phase 2 as an indication of the potential payback. It can be calculated again at the end of Phase 3, after the improvements have been implemented, to determine the actual payback.

Cash Flow Profile

The payback ratio measures only the eventual return; it does not identify when this return is achieved. The time factor is recognized in a cash flow profile, as illustrated by the actual case shown in Figure 13.2. The company invested in their O.F.A. program for the first three months, resulting in a continuous negative cash flow, both on an out-of-pocket and on a full-cost basis. During the fourth month, first improvements were implemented, and their savings began to offset the investment. In subsequent months, as further improvements were implemented, these savings grew, and the cash flow curve bent upward until all investment had been offset. As shown in Figure 13.2, this crossover occurred during the ninth month on an out-of-pocket cost basis, and after eleven months on a full-cost basis, savings continued to accumulate into the future. This organization achieved a payback ratio of 13.5 or 5.5 for the out-of-pocket or full cost case, respectively, typical for programs of this type.

SUMMARY

Let's take a few moments and see where we began, and where we are now. Early in this book, we read about the logic or theory of O.F.A. We learned that the participative, do-it-yourself approach was best. Lasting improvement must come from within and cannot

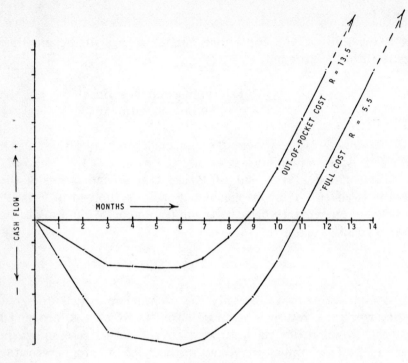

Figure 13.2

be imposed from the outside. We then identified a number of factors that lead to more effective participation, and illustrated them.

We then learned that real, lasting productivity improvement requires change, and change requires creativity and innovation. But we all are creatures of habit, with many old biases and preconceived notions. Chapter 3 identified some of these obstacles to innovation so we could recognize and overcome them. Therefore, the next chapter gave us some ideas on how to develop more creative attitudes and skills, both as individuals and as members of a group, such as an O.F.A. team.

We then read about the demands that impact an organization, and cause people within it to perform functions and operations to meet these demands. We learned that the productivity of an organization is determined by the characteristics of the demands placed on it, more than by any other factor. Lasting improvements can be achieved when we identify and remove those features of a demand that cause unnecessary, unproductive work.

After this we read about the interorganizational factor in productivity improvement. We learned that what appears to be a major problem in one department often is only a symptom of an even greater problem in another department. For this reason, 50–80% of the potential improvement in most organizations involves the work flow *between* departments.

Chapter 8 described the first phase of the typical O.F.A. method, senior management introduction and planning, during which senior management establishes the objectives, scope, participation, and schedules for the remainder of the O.F.A. program.

With Chapter 9, we moved into Phase 2 of the O.F.A. process, middle management analysis and recommendation. We read how the O.F.A. team was organized, and how it planned its work. We then read about information collection, the first of four steps that comprise Phase 2, during which the O.F.A. team members gather both quantitative and qualitative information on activities within the O.F.A. program scope.

However, the information collected is raw information, and must be analyzed before it can be used. During this second step, the O.F.A. team condenses the quantitative information to determine the effort and expense devoted to each major function performed in the organization. The team then condenses the qualitative information into a list of key observations.

Chapter 11 described the third step in Phase 2, evaluation and improvement identification. During this step, O.F.A. team members evaluate the information, and see what it really means. Based on these evaluations, they identify potential improvements and changes in the work flow that will make the organization more productive, and document these on observation and recommendation sheets.

In the fourth step, implementation planning and recommendation, the team members develop specific improvement recommendations, and document them on improvement project sheets. They then assign priorities to each project, and develop a time-phased implementation plan. Next, they prepare and present to senior management both written and oral reports containing these recommended improvements and implementation plans.

All of the foregoing work has led us to the final Phase 3, improvement implementation, described in the current chapter. In this phase, senior managers and O.F.A. team members work together to refine the initial implementation plans.

Related implementation projects are grouped, and each group assigned to a task force for implementation. Each task force is led by line managers responsible for the activities within the projects. Each senior manager is responsible for guiding and monitoring one or more task force.

Tangible benefits can be measured by both payback ratios and cash flow profiles to determine the economic gains associated with the O.F.A. program.

Now let's move on to the remaining chapters, which describe actual case studies that illustrate the logic and method of the O.F.A. process.

Part III
Case Studies Illustrating
Use of O.F.A.

Chapter 14
Demand Identification
Improves Productivity of
Order Handling Activities

Our first example is a small manufacturer of consumer products, selling for about $400 each, and used in suburban homes and farms. Although all customer orders were for essentially the same product, each order was tailored to meet a specific customer's needs by the addition of options and accessories. All sales were made and orders received through the U.S. Mail. Each customer order was processed individually through a head-end order handling department, after which it was released to the manufacturing department for fabrication and assembly and shipment by common carrier to the customer.

MANAGEMENT OBJECTIVE

Customer order receipt and shipment rates were very seasonal. Permanent employees in the manufacturing department handled the base load, and part-time employees absorbed the seasonal peaks.

For some unexplainable reason, the number of employees in the head-end order handling department remained essentially constant, at about 34 people, all working diligently. This surprised both the department and senior managers, who logically expected a seasonal variation.

Therefore, a major objective of the O.F.A. program was to develop a better way to forecast manpower requirements in the order handling department.

This department consisted of three sections: mail room, customer representatives, and data processing. All customer orders were received in the mail room and then sent to the customer reps. Here they were edited, acknowledged, logged, and launched into the process. They then went to data processing, where each order was entered into the computer-based monitoring and control system.

IDENTIFY THE DEMANDS

A small O.F.A. team was formed. The team members learned the O.F.A. process, and began their analysis. Their first step was to identify the major demands on their department. Their immediate response was that the major demand was the customer order. After all, their department was called *order* handling!

When the team members conducted interviews in the three sections, they discovered that there were *eight* significant demands on their department, as listed in Table 14.1.

Look at the table. What do you see? Is the customer order for a machine the principal demand? Well, for sure it is a significant demand, and 250 of them were received on the average day when this analysis was made. However, more than 5,000 other demands hit the organization on that same day!

Many customers sent only down payments with their machine orders, and later sent supplemental payments for the balance. In fact, since some customers sent more than one such payment, more supplemental payments were received than original orders.

Customers inquired about their in-house orders 120 times a day. They placed 100 orders for service parts, and 500 orders for books and instruction manuals.

Table 14.1. Analysis of Demands.

DEMAND	AVERAGE DAILY VOLUME
Machine orders	250
Supplemental payments on machine orders	320
Order inquiries to customer representatives	120
Service parts orders	100
Book orders	500
Requests for promotional literature	2,620
General mail	850
Editor mail	600

At the time of this program, over 2,600 requests were received each day for promotional literature describing the company's products and services.

Finally, 850 pieces of general mail were received each day, as well as 600 letters to the editor of a newsletter the company sent to its customers.

Clearly, this was a lot more than just an "order handling" department. There were many significant demands in addition to machine orders, and the activities were much more complex than the team members had anticipated.

IDENTIFY THE FUNCTIONS

The O.F.A. team then identified about 30 functions performed within the order handling department to meet these demands. Here is a partial list:

General mail handling. Receiving, opening, sorting, distributing incoming mail.

Promotional literature program. All activities involved in receiving and filling requests for promotional literature.

Order editing. Opening orders, verifying validity, identifying rejected orders, sending rejects to telephone sales for follow up.

Order control. Activities to ensure customer order forms and resulting paperwork do not get lost in processing, including counting, batching, total checks, etc.

Order monitoring. Activities to ensure that the machine order is processed through manufacturing and shipped to the customer on schedule.

Order entry. Preparation of data input sheets, key punching, and activities needed to get order into both computer files and customer folders.

Order acknowledgment. Informing customers their orders have been received, accepted, and are in process.

Payment collection. Reminding customer that he owes more money.

Payment Receiving. Receiving both original payments and supplemental payments, endorsing checks, "receiving" order forms, assigning cash receipt numbers, etc.

Manufacturing master scheduling. Assigning incoming orders into the current week's file, monitoring forecasted load in the current and future weeks, verifying this load against capacity.

COLLECT, ANALYZE INFORMATION

Once the team members had identified the principal demands and functions in the order handling department, they conducted information collection interviews with their colleagues in the three sections, mail room, customer representatives, and data processing.

Function Summary Sheets

The team members then analyzed this information, and derived a set of function summary sheets, one of which is shown in Figure 14.1.
   Look at that sheet. What do you see?

Promotional Literature Program

The single largest function performed in this department was the promotional literature program. Mail room people devoted 26% of their time to it, and the data processing section spent 74% of its time on it. The 71 hours (16.5 + 54.4 = 70.9) consumed by this one function was over one-fourth of all available time in the department! What do we have here, an order handling department, or an advertising department? What's the full story behind this function? The function summary sheet may not give us all the answers but it can surely lead us to ask the right questions.

Order Monitoring

The next largest function was order monitoring. Remember what that was? "Activities to ensure that the machine order is processed

OPERATION FUNCTION ANALYSIS

FUNCTION SUMMARY SHEET
ACTIVITIES: ORDER HANDLING

FUNC NO	FUNCTION DESCRIPTION	DEMAND DESCRIPTION	DEMAND VOLUME	TOTAL HOURS	MAIL ROOM HRS.	%	CUST. REPR. HRS.	%	DATA PROCESS. HRS.	%
1	Mail handling	Pieces	1450	10.5	10.5	16				
2	Promotional literature prog.	Requests	2620	70.9	16.5	26			54.4	74
3	Order editing - machine orders	Mach. orders	250	8.7	8.2	13	.5	-		
4	Order control - machine orders	Mach. orders	250	8.9	5.1	8	3.8	3		
5	Order monitoring - mach.ord.	Mach. orders	250	33.7			31.5	23	2.2	3
6	Order entry - machine orders	Mach. orders	250	13.8			11.0	8	2.8	4
7	Order acknowledgment - m.o.'s	Mach. orders	250	9.0			9.0	7		
8	Payment collection - m.o.'s	Mach. orders	250	9.0			9.0	7		
9	Payment receiving - m.o.'s	Mach. orders	250	6.0	3.6	6			2.4	3
10	Mfg. master sched'g. - m.o.'s	Mach. orders	250	1.5			1.5	1		
11	Mfg. short range sched'g - "	Mach. orders	250	6.0			6.0	4		
12	Order release - mach. orders	Mach. orders	250	18.5			18.5	14		
13	Order close-out - mach.orders	Mach. orders	250	2.0			2.0	2		
14	Order control - suppl.pymnts	Suppl.pymnts	320	1.7	1.7	3				
15	Payment collect. - suppl.pymt.	Suppl.pymnts	320	19.6			19.6	14		
16	Payment receiving - supp.pmt.	Suppl.pymnts	320	10.4	3.1	5	4.3	3	3.0	4
17	Order editing - service parts	Parts orders	100	3.3	3.3	5				

Figure 14.1

through manufacturing and shipped to the customer on schedule." Are you surprised that the head-end order handling department devoted over 30 hours every day monitoring the manufacturing department? This is nearly one-quarter of the time available in the customer representative section, and 12% of the time in the whole order handling department (33.7/272 = 0.12).

But wait. Is this really a problem in the order handling department, or is it a symptom of greater problems in the manufacturing planning and control section? Do we have a misplaced function? Why are the functions of order monitoring and manufacturing master scheduling performed in the order handling department, rather than in the manufacturing planning and control section, the traditional place for such activities? Does this indicate a need for major improvements in the manufacturing planning and control section?

Payment Collection and Receiving

Look further down on Figure 14.1. Notice that functions 8 and 9, payment collection and receiving for machine orders, consumed 15 hours per day. Yet collection and receiving for *supplemental payments,* functions 15 and 16, consumed twice that much. What does this tell us? Does this indicate a problem with collecting and receiving the supplemental payments?

A Basic Problem

Each customer order was placed in the order backlog as soon as received (function 6, Figure 14.1). However, it was released from the order handling department to the manufacturing department (function 12 in Figure 14.1) only after all supplemental payments were collected and received (functions 15 and 16).

Many collections were difficult, as indicated by the great amount of time devoted to functions 15 and 16. Furthermore, the timing of the receipt of these payments was uneven and unpredictable, and occurred in fits and spurts, according to the payment abilities of the customers.

This sent shock waves throughout the organization, as illustrated in Figure 14.2. Look at it. It is a perfect example of the old rule, what appears to be a problem in one organization, often is a symptom of a problem in another organization. In this case, from bottom up:

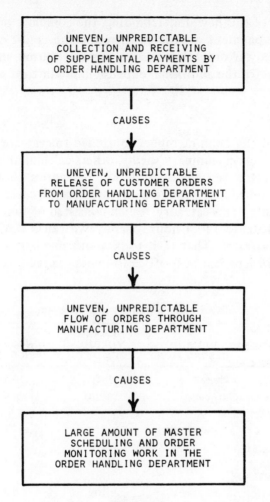

Figure 14.2

- The large amount of master scheduling in the order handling department was only a symptom of . . .
- Uneven, unpredictable order flow in manufacturing, which was a symptom of . . .
- Uneven, unpredictable release of customer orders from order handling into manufacturing, which was a symptom of . . .
- Uneven, unpredictable collection and receiving of supplemental payments by order handling.

As a result of this new understanding, the company phased out the supplemental payment approach, introduced a credit card payment plan, smoothed the order flow through manufacturing, and considered it all a bargain for the additional expense in credit card service fees.

O.F.A. Ratios

While some of the team members continued to evaluate the information on the function summary sheets, others calculated and evaluated O.F.A. ratios for ten major function categories shown in Table 14.2. They immediately focused on the second category, machine order processing. This category, which consisted of functions 3–13 in Figure 14.1, totalled 117.1 hours per day, with an O.F.A. ratio of 0.47 man-hours per order. That is, it took about one-half a man-hour to process each order from post office to release to manufacturing.

Table 14.2. Summary of Functions.

FUNCTION CATEGORY	DEMAND DESCRIPTION	DEMAND VOLUME PER DAY	MAN-HOURS PER DAY	O.F.A. RATIO
Mail handling	Pieces	1450	10.5	0.01
Promotional litera-ture program	Requests	2620	70.9	0.03
Machine order processing	Machine orders	250	117.1	0.47
Supplemental pay-ments processing	Payments	320	31.7	0.10
Service parts order processing	Parts orders	100	5.8	0.06
Book order processing	Book orders	500	4.3	0.01
Customer inquiries to customer reps	Inquiries	120	16.0	0.06
Changes in customer data			3.0	
General accounting			4.0	
Records maintenance			8.7	

How does that sound? Good, bad, so-so? Any questions you'd like to ask? What do you conclude? What does it mean?

Well, if you're like the O.F.A. team, it doesn't mean much. Just a number. But then they asked the crucial question: "Are all machine orders the same?"

The answer was obvious to the customer representatives involved in the program. "No. There are two types of machine orders, those with city addresses and those with rural addresses." The O.F.A. team members pursued it further and found out the following:

- About 75% of all customers lived in city suburbs with a typical address, such as "1559 S. Humbardt Avenue, Blattsville, North Dakota, 58989."
- The remaining 25% lived in the country, with a typical address, such as "Anjou Rd, RD #4, Box 76, Blattsville, North Dakota, 58989. Fourth white house north of junction of Anjou and railroad tracks." As indicated here, rural addresses typically included location and shipping information for the truck driver, in addition to the postal address.
- The system specialist who designed the order entry computer system was a "city boy," and knew little about country addresses. Hence, he reserved a space in the computer system for the customer address based on his understanding of city addresses.
- As a result, the computer system could not handle the larger country addresses, and separate manual records had to be maintained for these orders.
- Because of this, the average time to process a country address machine order was 1.05 hours, over four times as long as the 0.25 hours needed for a city address order!

Major Improvement

The O.F.A. team members suddenly realized that their review of these O.F.A. ratios had led them to a major potential improvement. All they had to do was change the computer program to accommodate the larger country addresses, and they, too, could be processed in about 0.25 hours. When this was done, the average time to process a machine order dropped from 0.47 hours to 0.25 hours, a dramatic 47% reduction in processing effort.

ORIGINAL MANAGEMENT OBJECTIVES

Senior managers wanted to understand the unexpected, constant level of people in the order handling department, and to develop a better way to forecast manpower levels in that organization.

During the program, the O.F.A. team members identified a number of potential productivity improvements, and this was excellent. But what happened to the original management objectives?

Constant Manpower Levels

Why did the order handling department always have about the same number of diligently working people, despite the fluctuating load of customer orders?

O.F.A. team members realized that the department's many activities fell into three broad groups, each following a separate time pattern or cycle.

- *Cycle 1.* Those activities related to and moving with the receipt and processing of customer machine orders.
- *Cycle 2.* Those activities that moved in a cycle approximately opposite, or 180 degrees out of phase with the cycle 1 group.
- *Constant.* Those activities that remained relatively constant throughout the year.

The composition of each group is shown in Table 14.3.

The O.F.A. program was conducted during the off season, and the order rate for machines was low. However, the volume of inquires for promotional literature was high, due to the heavy advertising program.

Soon the order rate would begin its seasonal increase, rising to about 50% greater than at the time of the program, with a corresponding increase in effort to 247 man-hours per day (164.8 X 1.5 = 247).

As the order rate rose, the advertising program would be reduced, and the effort to handle the requests for promotional literature would fall from the 71 hours per day shown in Table 14.3, to practically nothing, say 5 or 10 hours per day. At this point, the total required manpower would be 289 man-hours per day (247 + 16 + 26 = 289), essentially the same as in the off season, the time of their O.F.A. program.

Table 14.3. Functional Effort Categorized by Time Cycle.

FUNCTION CATEGORY	MAN-HOURS PER DAY		
	CYCLE 1	CYCLE 2	CONSTANT
Mail handling			10.5
Promotional literature program		70.9	
Machine order processing	117.1		
Supplemental payments processing	31.7		
Service parts order processing		5.8	
Book order processing		4.3	
Customer inquiries to customer reps	16.0		
Changes in customer data			3.0
General accounting			4.0
Records maintenance			8.7
	164.8	81.0	26.2

Later, as this high season peaked and passed, the order rate would fall, the advertising campaigns would start again, the rate of inquiries for promotional literature would rise, and the order handling department would return to the conditions that existed at the time of the O.F.A. program, about 272 man-hours per day, or 34 people. To be sure, there were temporary fluctuations throughout the year, and these were met with short-term temporary employees. But by and large, the number of permanent people in the order handling department remained the same.

Forecasting Manpower Requirements

Once the O.F.A. team arrived at this point, the rest was relatively simple. The marketing managers would prepare a rolling annual forecast by quarters for the following six factors:

1. Requests for promotional literature, based on economic trends and anticipated level of advertising
2. Customer machine orders, based on economic trends and anticipated sales programs
3. Supplemental payments, based on the number of machine orders expected and the collection and receiving methods in

use, recognizing such things as the phased introduction of credit card billing

4. Customer parts orders, based on the population of operating machine in use by customers

5. Book orders, largely based on past trends and anticipated promotions

6. Customer inquiries, based on customer order volume.

With this forecast in hand, the manager of the order handling department could multiply each of the six factors by the appropriate O.F.A. ratio from Table 14.2 and immediately determine the required manpower by quarter. In fact, he used a different set of O.F.A. ratios for each of the three sections, mail room, customer representatives, and data processing, and thereby was able to forecast manpower needs by section, as well as total manpower needs by department. Furthermore, the O.F.A. ratios were changed to reflect modifications in operating practices expected to occur in the following year.

SUMMARY

This was a complex little case study, and it contained a number of lessons.

Although at first, the O.F.A. team recognized only one demand, machine orders, they soon realized that seven other major demands had significant impacts on the department's effort and productivity, and that each should be evaluated.

Through a review of major functions, they then exposed problems in order handling, that were symptoms of problems in manufacturing, which in turn were symptoms of problems back in order handling. By breaking this loop, they achieved significant improvements.

Using their O.F.A. ratios, they identified major differences in the effort required to process country orders versus city orders. Although these demands could not be changed, the process for handling could be, with major productivity improvements.

Finally, using these same O.F.A. ratios, they were able to explain why the manpower in the order handling department remained essentially constant, and were also able to establish a new method for forecasting this manpower by section within the department.

Chapter 15
Analysis of Alternate Routes in Engineering Improves Overall Company Productivity

This case is very different from the first one and involves a major manufacturer of large mechanical equipment. Each customer order was for a set of integrated equipment composed of several modules. All orders were individually engineered. A few orders were totally new designs. Most orders involved major adaptations and rearrangements of components used on earlier orders. An occasional order was essentially a duplicate of an earlier one. Total order processing cycle time ranged from one to four years, depending on the complexity of the design and the size of the modules comprising the customer order.

MANAGEMENT OBJECTIVE

As one element in the total O.F.A. program, management wished to determine the impact of the complexity of the product design on (1) the engineering effort in particular, and (2) the business in general.

Engineers had always recognized that some customer orders required more and some less engineering effort. However, they viewed their activities as a monolithic block — "engineering." They did not formally divide their work into different engineering functions, nor did they recognize alternate routes through these functions. hence, they had little way of analyzing, forecasting, or measuring the relative effort devoted to any given order.

ALTERNATE ROUTES

With analysis, they identified nine principal engineering functions, connected by alternate routes, as illustrated in Figure 15.1. Depending on the requirements, and the resulting design characteristics, each customer order passed through one of these different routes.

Every module for a customer order passed through the first three functions. In preliminary specification and final specification functions, the engineers studied the customer requirements, and identified what engineering would be needed to meet these requirements. In the O.F.A. language, they identified the features of the demand (customer order). Based on these features, they then were able to schedule the module in question through one of five possible alternate routes in the engineering organization.

Route 5. If the module in the customer order required a totally new design, then it passed through advance engineering, where new design concepts were created. It then passed to development engineering, where these concepts were firmed up, and the basic design developed. It next went through preliminary design, design revision, and finally into engineering documentation, where drawings and bills of material were prepared. In the engineering release function, this documentation was distributed to the manufacturing organization.

Route 4. If the customer specifications for the module did not require totally new concepts, the order would short circuit advance engineering, pass directly to development engineering, and then flow down through the rest of the engineering functions.

Route 3. If the module in the order could be based on a combination of new design work, along with major redesign and rearrangement of components from previous designs, it then would follow a path directly to preliminary design, and on through the rest of the functions.

Route 2. If the module required only a redesign and rearrangement of known components, then it went directly to design revision and on.

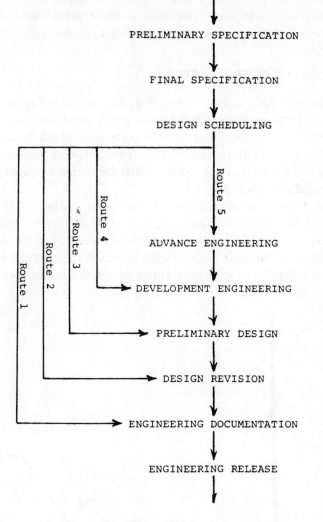

Figure 15.1

Route 1. In those very few cases in which the customer order duplicated an earlier one, then the module would pass directly to engineering documentation and on through engineering release.

IMPACT ON ENGINEERING EFFORT

By analyzing the relative effort assigned to each function for the preceding year, and identifying how many modules passed through each route for the same period, the people involved in this program were able to calculate the O.F.A. ratios for each function, and determine the relative engineering effort for each alternate route. The results are shown in Figure 15.2.

Route 1 represented the easiest route, going directly from design scheduling to engineering documentation, and was assigned a relative effort of 1. Route 5 was the most difficult because each order module passed through all engineering functions. Figure 15.2 shows the results for three different types of product modules. Modules

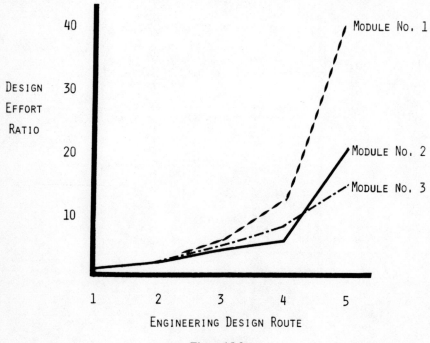

Figure 15.2

that passed through route 5 consumed from 15–40 times as much engineering effort as those that passed through route 1.

As indicated earlier, very few orders went through either route 1 or route 5. For example, a module 1 passed through route 5 only about once every 7–10 years. Most modules passed through routes 2, 3, and 4. Yet even within this range, the relative effort between route 2 and route 4 increased significantly.

IMPACT ON OTHER ACTIVITIES

The team pursued this further. They examined the impact that these same module designs had on indirect activities within the manufacturing organizations. When engineers passed the order through the longer, more complex routes, they created newness, and this newness caused additional work in the downstream organizations. For example, Figure 15.3 shows that a module that passed through route 5 required more production control effort than one passing

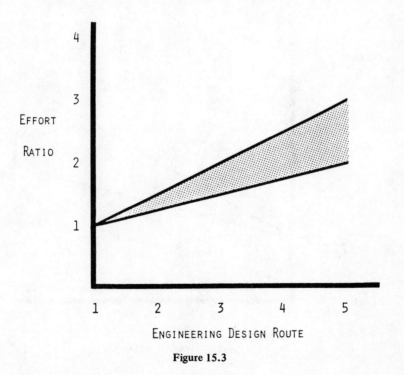

Figure 15.3

through route 1 by a factor of at least 2 : 1, since every new component required new operation and routing information, schedule information, etc.

The team also examined the impact that this same newness had on the cost accounting organization. Every new component required a new cost calculation, and this resulted in increased cost accounting effort, as shown in Figure 15.4.

RESULTS OF O.F.A. STUDY

When the team presented these preliminary results to engineering management, they heard what they expected to hear. That is, although engineering people had some influence over the route through which an order module would pass, it was really the sales staff that had the greatest influence. If they were able to sell a customer on a product configuration similar to an earlier design, the

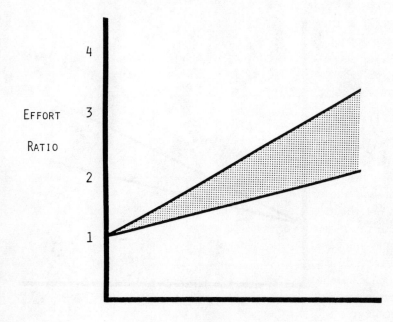

Figure 15.4

engineers could meet the customer requirements through route 2. On the other hand, if the sales people sold a customer a product configuration that was very new, then the order would by necessity pass through route 4 or even route 5.

The team members then met with sales management and presented their story. The sales manager replied:

> Impossible. Your numbers are wrong, and I can prove it. Engineering costs are about the same for each type of product, regardless of the design newness and complexity. It doesn't make much difference what we sell, the engineers spend about the same amount of time on each order.
>
> Here, look at these order recap sheets that show the price received from the customer, and the costs incurred on each order. I get a sheet on every order we ship. We've gotten them for years.
>
> Take these two orders for example. They are the same general product type and rating. The first one was essentially a new design. I remember. I sold it myself. However, the second was nearly a duplicate of the first, and required essentially no new engineering.
>
> But look, the engineering costs on these two recap sheets are nearly the same. This proves that engineering costs are about the same for each type of product, regardless of the design newness required by the customer specifications.

The sales manager had fallen into an old trap. He misunderstood accounting information. Recap sheets were issued as general financial guides, not as a basis for order pricing evaluations. Factory direct labor and material costs on these recap sheets were accurate. However, overhead costs, including engineering, were allocated to orders based on a percentage of factory labor and material. Hence the engineering costs on the recap sheets were totally unreliable.

How did all this end up? Clearly, in a heavy equipment business, the salesman must respond to the needs of the customers. To do otherwise would lose the order. Nevertheless, every salesman has some degree of latitude within which he can influence the customer, and even slight changes in customer requirements could greatly simplify the design process, with major savings in effort in engineering and other departments.

SUMMARY

In this O.F.A. program, the team members quickly learned the importance of:

Alternate routes
Demand characteristics
O.F.A. ratios
Demand modification.

They identified five alternate routes through the design engineering processes. The characteristics of the products specified on a customer order determined the route through which the order would flow. By calculating O.F.A. ratios, they determined the relative effort for each route, and exposed major differences, both for the engineering activities and other downstream work. Furthermore, they now could measure, analyze, and forecast engineering loads based on these product features.

Chapter 16
O.F.A. in Production
Planning and Control

This typical business produces and distributes medium-size equipment to other businesses and government agencies. Earlier management reviews exposed a number of "factory problems," including the following:

- They continually struggled to meet the monthly "sales billed" budget.
- The factory consistently produced significantly less than the required master schedule, even though resources appeared adequate.
- Product quality was less than desired, despite large quality assurance efforts.
- Farmouts had increased, with resulting cost increases.
- Unfavorable direct labor cost variances were increasing.

MANAGEMENT OBJECTIVES

These appear to be traditional factory problems. Or were they really only symptoms of greater problems in other organizations?

Company senior executives established an interdisciplinary O.F.A. team to:

- Clearly identify the real, root problems
- Develop ways to correct these problems and improve the productivity of their business.

Here are some of the things they discovered.

BUSINESS WORK FLOW

In theory, the business should have operated with a formal system as shown in the solid lines in Figure 16.1, and senior managers believed this was happening. The production and material planning and control department should have evaluated market forecasts against finished goods inventory levels and production plans, and then triggered off material and labor activities to meet forecasted require-

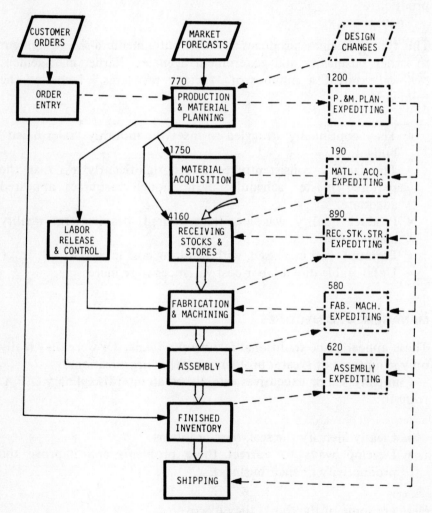

Figure 16.1

ments. The order entry organization should have received customer orders, and drawn from the finished inventory to meet them.

Through their program, the O.F.A. team established that the business actually operated with the added processes shown by the dotted lines in Figure 16.1. Market forecasts still were received and used by production and material planning and control as a basis for replenishing the finished goods inventory. However, when order entry sought to fill customer orders, they would find that proper products were not available in the inventory.

They would override the formal system, and place these customer requirements directly on production and material planning and control, which then would initiate the complex, informal, special expediting activities shown on the right of Figure 16.1.

The O.F.A. team recognized this special expediting was a great drain on the business, and probably was a symptom of problems elsewhere. They continued their O.F.A. evaluation to:

- Quantify the magnitude of the expediting effort
- Define the basic problems that caused it
- Identify ways to correct these problems.

EXPEDITING

The O.F.A. team reviewed data from its information collection and analysis steps, and found that a large amount of expediting occurred in several organizations, as shown in Figure 16.1, and summarized in Table 16.1.

Table 16.1. Expediting.

ORGANIZATION	MAN-HOURS PER MONTH
Production and material planning and control	1,200
Material acquisition	190
Receiving, stocks, and stores	890
Fabrication and machining	580
Assembly	620
Total	3,480

Older, traditional simplification methods would have sought simply to speed up this expediting. However, the team members used the O.F.A. approach and asked:

- Do 3,480 hours per month for expediting constitute a reasonable level of activity?
- Why is this expediting necessary?
- Is it unproductive work?
- What demands cause these activities?
- How can we change the demands to reduce this work?

FORWARD PLANNING VERSUS EXPEDITING

The O.F.A. team members set out to answer the first question. They recognized that every company does some expediting. Perhaps they were doing only a reasonable, normal amount. To evaluate this, the team reviewed its data. They found that 770 man-hours per month were applied to the formal, top-down, forward-oriented planning functions shown in Table 16.2.

Team members then realized that the bottom-up expediting effort exceeded the top-down forward planning effort by ratio of 4.5 : 1, clearly an undesirable condition (3,480/770 = 4.51).

Even worse, the expediting effort exceeded the real planning effort, 80 hours for master scheduling and 30 for inventory planning, by a factor of over 30 : 1! The team suddenly realized why they were doing an increasing amount of expediting. Bottom-up hot listing, not forward planning, was driving the business.

Table 16.2. Forward Planning Functions.

FUNCTION	MAN-HOURS PER MONTH
Master scheduling	80
Inventory planning	30
Resource planning	110
Fabrication and machining scheduling	370
Assembly scheduling	180
Total	770

From this initial review of their O.F.A. data, they recognized that expediting was a widespread problem, involving a number of organizations, and consuming an outlandish amount of time. Furthermore, they had the data to back up their conclusions.

Why was this widespread expediting necessary? What demands really caused it? What could be done to reduce it? The team addressed these questions. Further review of the function summary sheets showed that the 3,480 hours per month devoted to expediting shown in Table 16.1 could be divided into two broad categories:

1. 1,460 hours devoted to expediting the materials *to* the factory floor
2. 2,020 hours consumed by expediting activities *on* the factory floor itself.

FACTORY FLOOR EXPEDITING

The team focused on the functions within the larger category, as listed in Table 16.3. They realized that the preparation, monitoring, and expediting of factory hot lists consumed 1,430 hours per month, which equals 71% of factory floor expediting, or 41% of all expediting.

In addition to these 1,430 hours, the hot list mode caused continual changes in work assignments, short production runs, and excessive

Table 16.3. Factory Floor Expediting Functions.

FUNCTION	MAN-HOURS PER MONTH
Hot list preparation	370
Hot list monitoring	200
Hot list expediting	860
Service parts expediting	330
Tool expediting	200
Manpower expediting	40
Lost equipment expediting	20
Total	2,020

teardown and setup, all of which resulted in increased direct and indirect labor and quality assurance expenses.

Why did this great amount of factory floor expediting occur? Based on their study, the Team members concluded it occurred for three reasons:

1. *Inadequate master scheduling.* Table 16.2 shows only 80 hours per month for this function. This was supported by even less market forecasting effort.
2. *Inadequate capacity planning.* Their computerized planning system did not have an effective resource planning module. Only 110 hours per month were devoted to manual resource planning, as shown in Table 16.2. By necessity, factory work stations were scheduled on informal, continually changing hot lists.
3. *Design changes.* Unilateral design decisions were made by engineering and placed on manufacturing without adequate lead times.

The O.F.A. team concluded that essentially all factory floor expediting was a symptom, caused by problems in other department, principally market forecasting, production planning, and design engineering.

MATERIAL EXPEDITING

The team then turned its attention to material expediting, and examined the functions that comprised this category, as shown in Table 16.4. They immediately recognized that 1,000 hours per month were devoted to investigating and physically searching for "lost" raw materials and production parts; this consumed 68% of material expediting time, and 29% of all expediting time. An equivalent of more than six people in this organization were continually looking for "lost" materials!

Although material expediting was shared by many people, including key managers, 1,080 out of the 1,460 hours occurred in two departments, as shown in Figure 16.1: material acquisition (190 hours per month) and receiving, stocks, and stores (890 hours per month).

Table 16.4. Material Expediting Functions.

FUNCTION	MAN-HOURS PER MONTH
Shipments expediting	60
Outside pickups	340
Receiving expediting	30
Raw material expediting	30
"Lost" raw material search	240
"Lost" production parts investigation	320
"Lost" production parts search	440
Total	1,460

Why was this material lost? What could be done to prevent this, and save the unproductive effort? What was happening within the material acquisition and receiving, stocks, and stores departments that would cause this high level of expediting, especially for "lost" materials?

Receiving, Stocks, and Stores

To answer these questions, the team focused on this larger block of work. As shown in Figure 16.1, the business devoted 4,160 man-hours per month to these activities; the functions in question are listed in Table 16.5.

Raw Material Withdrawal

The team immediately spotted the 690 hours per month devoted to withdrawing raw materials from inventory prior to release to the factory floor. This appeared excessive. Further investigation identified that this function was made up of three groups of operations, shown in Table 16.6.

Team members checked back through their interview notes and key observations, and discovered that when the inventory clerks reviewed their records for material availability, as much as 50% of all data displayed through their computer terminals was in error! Here was one source of "lost" material. The materials weren't physically

Table 16.5. Receiving, Stocks, and Stores Functions.

FUNCTION	MAN-HOURS PER MONTH
Raw material receiving	230
Raw material withdrawal	690
Production parts receiving	640
Production parts withdrawal	2,020
General receiving	580
Total	4,160

Table 16.6. Raw Material Withdrawal.

GROUP OF OPERATIONS	MAN-HOURS PER MONTH
Review inventory records for material availability	170
Special search for lost materials	180
Move to first work station	340
Total	690

lost; rather, they were lost on the computer records. This resulted in the following unnecessary and unproductive work:

- The team estimated that at least 85 out of the 170 hours devoted to reviewing inventory records were unnecessary.
- All 180 hours per month consumed by the special search for "lost" materials was totally unproductive and unnecessary.
- Key observations indicated that 75% of all material moved from the raw material storage area to the first work station required special handling at the time of withdrawal, and as a result, at least one-third of the 340 hours devoted to this, or 113 hours, were unnecessary.

Based on these observations, team members concluded that data errors in the raw material inventory system resulted in approximately 378 hours a month direct loss in the three activities mentioned above (85 + 180 + 113 = 378). When they added this to the 30 hours per month devoted to raw material expediting and 240 hours for lost raw material search shown in Table 16.4, team members realized that a total of 648 man-hours per month of unnecessary, unproductive work occurred because of these data errors (378 + 30 + 240 = 648).

Clearly, one of the principal causes of excessive material expediting was data errors in the inventory system. Why?

Raw Material Receiving

Turning their attention to the raw material receiving activities, which consumed 230 hours per month (Table 16.5), they found two things:

1. The material receiving crews had to convert units of measure for much of the raw material received. For example, material was received by weight, yet inventory records were kept in length. As they converted records, errors were made, as might be expected. These errors were entered into the computer raw material inventory control system, and resulted in "lost" materials.
2. The storage racks in the raw material receiving areas were inadequate. Material was stacked as received, which resulted in physically lost materials, and required 75% special handling when moved to the first work station.

At last, a great distance from where they began, the O.F.A. team found the basic causes for the excessive material expediting: inaccurate data input, inadequate storage racks.

Material receiving clerks were provided with hand calculators to use as they converted the units of measure of incoming raw materials, thus sharply reducing the data input errors. Simple changes and extensions were made to the raw material storage racks, clearing up the problem of physically lost materials in that area. Together, these rather modest, even unexciting changes resulted in savings of several hundred hours per month.

Production Parts Withdrawal

The team members then concentrated on the production parts withdrawal activities, which consumed 2,020 hours per month, as shown in table 16.5.

In theory, the production planning system released requisitions to the production parts inventory areas, ordering parts to be moved in proper-size lots to factory floor assembly areas.

In practice, it did not work that way. The team members found that the great majority of requisitions for production parts were transmitted directly from the factory assembly area to the stocks and stores office, by telephone, as a result of continual, last minute expediting on the factory floor.

An inventory clerk would check his computer terminal to determine the availability of the requested part. If the part was there, the clerk sent the stock delivery attendant to get and deliver the part to the production floor.

However, roughly 50% of the time the stock attendant could not find the requested part in the required volume. The computer inventory record showed a larger on-hand quantity then was actually in inventory. Again, lost parts.

Why were these production parts and subassemblies lost? To answer this, the team members reviewed the interview notes for the production parts inventory areas and remembered the following:

- Because of the continual expedite mode on the factory floor, and the telephone requests for stock part transfers, production parts were withdrawn and sent to the assembly lines in "bulk" in their storage containers, rather than the net quantity shown on the assembly bill of material. The bulk amount would be deducted from the inventory records by the inventory clerks. If this reduced the inventory record sufficiently, a requisition would be sent to purchasing for more material, and a purchase order sent to the vendor.

- The assembly crews used as many parts as needed from the bulk container, and returned the remainder, uncounted, to inventory storage. The remainder was credited to the inventory record based on the planned usage of the part, even though the actual usage often was significantly larger because of misuse, waste, etc. In many cases, this credit would restore the inventory record to a sufficient level, and the system would cancel the purchase order just sent to the vendor. This tangle of records was another source of lost materials.

Production Parts Receiving

Still searching for other reasons for lost production parts, the team members reexamined the results of their interviews in the production parts receiving activities. They found no physical counts were made at the time of receiving. Instead, the receiving clerks merely accepted the count shown on the incoming papers. Many errors occurred. Another source of lost parts and subassemblies.

Based on their evaluation of the production parts activities, the O.F.A. team recommended more thorough physical counting procedures both when the parts were received from the vendor, and when they were transferred between the production parts inventory areas and the factory floor assembly areas. Although this increased the effort required in these two areas, it dramatically reduced the 2,020 hours per month devoted to production parts withdrawal (Table 16.5), the 320 hours for lost production parts investigation, and the 440 hours consumed by the lost production parts search (Table 16.4).

Material Acquisition

Early in their study, remember that the O.F.A. team recognized that most of the material expediting occurred in two broad areas: Receiving, stocks and, stores; and material acquisition. They now focused on this latter area, which consumed 190 man-hours per month (Figure 16.1). Why was this expediting necessary? What activities occurred in the material acquisition area that caused this expediting?

The O.F.A. team members reviewed their function summary sheets for purchasing, and located the information shown in Table 16.7.

Vendor Selection

One thing struck the team immediately. Purchasing was so busy handling purchase requisitions and orders that they spent no time in vendor evaluation and selection. This had to be corrected immediately. Let's see how they did it.

Requisition Evaluation

The team reviewed the function of purchase requisition evaluation, and found that out of the 530 hours per month, 440 hours were devoted to unproductive work, as shown in Table 16.8.

Why did the buyers in purchasing need to verify the validity of incoming material purchase requisitions and inventory balances? During their interviews, team members discovered that:

- 62% of all requisitions received by purchasing were requests for "fresh" purchase orders
- 38% of all requisitions were to change earlier purchase orders.

Consequently, about 38% of the 690 hours per month devoted to purchase order preparation (Table 16.7), or 262 hours, was unnecessary and unproductive. This was the equivalent of one or two people who could devote their effort to vendor evaluation and selection, if they could find a way to reduce the 38% volume of purchase order changes.

Why were these purchase orders changed so much? The team members continued and found that:

- 21% of the change requisitions cancelled existing purchase orders
- 11% of the change requisitions rescheduled existing purchase orders
- 25% expedited existing purchase orders
- 43% corrected errors in existing purchase orders.

Clearly, the problems leading to the widespread expediting and the lost material situation also continually churned the material acquisition process, and had a very adverse impact on the effectiveness of the purchasing department and its relationships with its vendors.

In fact, the team found it was worse than it first appeared. They stratified their data on purchase order cancellation and change notices. The results, shown in Table 16.9, showed that a great part of the changes, cancellations, and expediting in the material acquisition areas was devoted to C and D inventory items, the low-value, standard hardware material that clearly did not warrant such continual change.

Let's go back to the original question: "Why did the buyers in purchasing need to devote 440 hours per month to verifying the validity of incoming purchase requisitions and on-hand inventory balances?"

You can now see for yourself: 38% of the incoming requisitions involved changes to previously released purchase orders — cancella-

Table 16.7. Material Acquisition Functions.

FUNCTION	MAN-HOURS PER MONTH
Selection of vendors	0
Purchase requisition evaluation	530
Purchase order preparation	690
Purchase order monitoring	310
Farmout purchasing	220
Total	1,750

Table 16.8. Unproductive Work in Requisition Evaluation.

OPERATIONS	MAN-HOURS PER MONTH
Verify validity of incoming material purchase requisitions	190
Verify on-hand inventory balances	250
Total	440

Table 16.9. Purchase Order Cancellation and Expedite Notices.

INVENTORY CLASS	PERCENT OF CANCELLATION NOTICES	PERCENT OF EXPEDITE NOTICES
A	21	21
B	36	32
C	33	39
D	10	8

tions, reschedules, expedites, corrections. Furthermore, nearly 50% of these changes involved small-value items in the C and D inventory categories. Clearly, the buyers had to review each requisition to determine if the requested changes were sufficiently valid and substantive to warrant reissuing the purchase order. This consumed 190 man-hours per month.

The buyers also knew about the many problems associated with both the raw material and production parts inventory processes. They had little faith in many of the inventory records. When they received a requisition for a major purchase of material, they felt compelled to leave their office, go to the inventory storage areas, or the assembly floor, and verify the on-hand balances. This consumed another 250 hours per month, for a total of 440 hours, as shown in Table 16.8.

These 440 hours per month were unnecessary and unproductive, and were caused by the expedite mode in the factory, and the bad data in the computer inventory system. Once these problems were solved, as described earlier, the great bulk of these 440 hours could be eliminated. This could be added to the 262 hours potential savings in purchase order preparation mentioned before, for a total savings of 702 man-hours per month. Buyers and other people in purchasing could then devote much of this same time to the evaluation and selection of vendors, a very important task for which they had no time before the O.F.A. program.

Farmouts

The team also touched on the farmout situation. Through their interviews, they learned that there were 200 farmout orders each month, consuming 220 man-hours in the purchasing department alone.

Essentially all of these were due to the expedite mode of operation, and not from basic facility limitations. In addition to these 220 hours, farmouts resulted in high direct cost variances.

SUMMARY

What really caused the "factory floor" problems outlined at the beginning of this case study?

First, although the formal production and material planning and control system could be improved, it was essentially sound.

However, weak market forecasting, master scheduling, and inventory and capacity planning, along with frequent design changes, all resulted in the deterioration of the formal, top-down, forward oriented, production and material planning and control system.

To survive, factory floor management introduced an informal, bottom-up, hot list expediting procedure.

This situation was exacerbated by a "lost" material problem. In fact, little material was really physically lost; it was only lost as far as the formal inventory system was concerned. This in turn was largely due to lack of respect for the formal system, e.g., poor data input and poor physical control over material entering and leaving the inventory areas.

In addition to causing a great burden of thousands of man-hours per month of unproductive hot listing and expediting, these basic problems increased indirect effort in all aspects of material acquisition, stocking, and storing, and led to inefficient and unproductive use of direct labor on the factory floor.

In short, the "factory floor" problems were essentially all due to extraordinary demands placed on that department by surrounding organizations. The majority of these demands resulted from misuse of existing systems, not from flaws in the systems.

Chapter 17
Analysis in Purchasing
Department Leads to
Broad Improvement

For many years, a major manufacturer of medium-size electrical equipment had enjoyed strong customer loyalty based on excellent technical leadership. However, in the past year or two, they had missed their shipping schedules with increasing frequency. As a result, some of their best customers were forced to give their orders to competitors with more reliable shipping performances.

MANAGEMENT OBJECTIVES

Senior managers decided to conduct an O.F.A. program with many broad productivity objectives, including the improvement of their shipping performance. Since the principal problems appeared to be in the main line processing of customer orders, they decided to exclude the purchasing department from the program scope, along with several other support groups. O.F.A. team members, being closer to the details, reversed this decision, and urged that all these groups be include in the program, which was done.

PURCHASING ACTIVITIES

The O.F.A. team collected information in purchasing, analyzed it, and found a general work flow as illustrated in Figure 17.1, with effort devoted to twelve functions as listed in Table 17.1.

The O.F.A. team members were pleased to see the relatively large amount of time devoted to the first function, vendor evaluation and selection, since this should be a major duty of any purchasing organi-

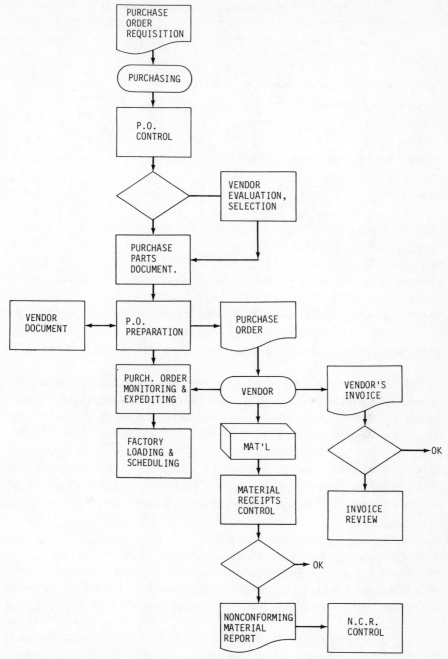

Figure 17.1

Table 17.1. Purchasing Department Functions.

OPERATION	MAN-HOURS PER MONTH	PERCENT
Vendor evaluation and selection	665	38.1
Purchase order monitoring and expediting	365	20.9
Purchase order preparation	274	15.7
Nonconforming material report control	168	9.6
Purchase parts documentation	97	5.5
Invoicing and collection	62	3.6
General clerical work	54	3.1
Material receipts control	29	1.7
Factory loading and scheduling	16	0.9
Purchase order control	8	0.5
Operations measurement	6	0.3
Vendor documentation	2	0.1

zation. However, they were quite disturbed to see that over 20% of the department's total effort was consumed by the second function, purchase order monitoring and expediting. They focused on this function.

At first, the team members followed the traditional approach to productivity improvement, that is, attack head on and find ways to speed up the process. They reviewed their interview data and saw that three operations made up 99% of the function:

- *Identify status of open purchase orders.* During this operation, buyers and purchasing analysts reviewed computer reports of open purchase orders and identified those which needed expediting.
  Effort: 91 hours per month
  Volume: 3,700 open orders per month
  O.F.A. ratio: 1.5 minutes per each open order.
- *Contact vendor to expedite order.* Buyers and analysts contacted vendors for information on purchase orders and expedited as necessary.
  Effort: 174 hours per month
  Volume: 385 orders expedited per month
  O.F.A. ratio: 27 minutes per expedite.

- *Input information to update system.* Buyers and analysts prepared data input sheets showing changes to purchase order status.
  Effort: 96 hours per month
  Volume: 2,440 updates per month
  O.F.A. ratio: 2.4 minutes per update.

Team members immediately recognized that this function could be performed more rapidly with an on-line computer system, and estimated these significant savings:

- One-third reduction in status review:
  91 X 0.33 = 30 hours per month
- One-fifth reduction in customer contact:
  174 X 0.2 = 35 hours per month
- One-half reduction in system update and input:
  96 X 0.5 = 48 hours per month.

The total of the three, 113 hours, was a reduction of 31% of the effort devoted to this function of purchase order monitoring and expediting, and a 6% reduction in the total effort of the purchasing department. The team was pleased with its results.

Identify Demands

At this point, the team members realized they were committing the traditional error, that is, simply speeding up unnecessary work. They remembered the basic step in O.F.A.: identify and modify demands. Working with people from purchasing, team members looked at their interview notes and key observations and established these facts:

- The purchasing department devoted a great amount of effort to order monitoring and expediting because vendors frequently shipped materials late, and missed the company's due dates.
- However, this usually was *not* the fault of the vendors. Most late shipments occurred because purchasing sent the purchase order late to the vendor, so late that no amount of extra effort by that vendor, nor monitoring and expediting by purchasing, could accelerate the process and get the materials in on time.

- Why did purchasing send the orders late? Surely not through lack of interest or effort. Purchase order preparation was their third largest function, consuming 274 hours per month, as shown in Table 17.1.

- In fact, purchasing sent the *orders* late because they received the   *requisitions* late. Other departments sent requisitions to purchasing instructing them to issue orders for required materials. Investigation showed that, on average, 20% percent of these requisitions were already late when received by purchasing — a very large volume in this type of business. Regardless of the effort they devoted to the function of purchase order preparation, the buyers and analysts could not issue the purchase orders on time to the vendors.

At last, the O.F.A. team members identified the basic demand that caused the great amount of monitoring and expediting effort, that is, late requisitions received from other departments.

Late Requisitions

How big was this problem? How late were these requisitions? Were some later than others? What was the impact of various degrees of lateness? What potential improvement might be achieved if fewer of them were late?

With the help of the O.F.A. team, people in Purchasing derived the curve in Figure 17.2. For example, if the normal ordering and delivery cycle time for a component was 60 days, but only 48 remained when purchasing received the requisition, then the requisition was twelve days, or 20% late (12/60 = 0.20). Figure 17.2 shows that the buyers and analysts would need about two hours of monitoring and expediting to improve this lateness. These were only estimates, but they were made by the best informed people, the ones who did the work.

The purchasing people immediately pointed out that lateness fluctuated throughout the year. Sometimes there was more lateness,

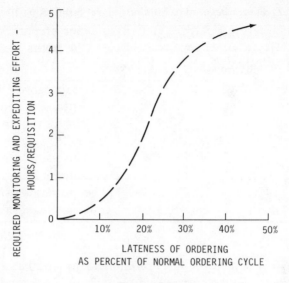

Figure 17.2

and they did more monitoring and expediting. Other times, perhaps several months later, there was less. At the time of the O.F.A. program, lateness was about average.

Impact of Lateness

The team therefore based their evaluation on three levels of lateness (low, medium and high), and calculated the data shown in Table 17.2.

For instance, they estimated that at a medium level of requisition lateness, 80% of the requisitions arrived in purchasing on time, hence required no monitoring nor expediting; 12% of the requisitions arrived 10% late and required 0.4 hours of monitoring and expediting for each requisition; 5% arrived 20% late, and each required 2.0 hours of monitoring and expediting; etc.

Based on the data in Table 17.2, and an average monthly volume of requisitions, the team calculated that 150 man-hours a month would be required for monitoring and expediting at a low level of

Table 17.2. Effort Devoted to Purchase Order Monitoring and Expediting

PERCENT VOLUME OF ORDERS			PERCENT LATE	MAN-HOURS EFFORT
LOW LATENESS	MEDIUM LATENESS	HIGH LATENESS		
90	80	70	not late	0.0
7	12	16	10	0.4
2	5	8	20	2.0
1	2	4	30	3.8
0	1	2	40	4.4
150	370	650	◄——— Man-hours per month	
11	26	45	◄——— Percent total effort	

lateness, 370 at a medium level of lateness, and 650 at a high level of lateness. These values corresponded to 11%, 26%, and 45% of the total effort in the purchasing department. The team and the people in purchasing were satisfied with these numbers because the 370 hours per month in Table 17.2 agreed very well with the 365 hours originally derived through their interviews.

Potential Improvement

They realized that if something could be done to reduce the level of lateness, major savings in effort could be achieved. For instance, if they could find a way to move from a medium level of lateness to a low level, purchasing could save 220 man-hours per month, nearly twice that which could be saved through the introduction of an on-line computer system mentioned earlier!

Furthermore, they had exposed and quantified a potential danger. If the level of lateness moved from medium to high, the monitoring and expediting effort would increase to 650 man-hours per month, or 45% of the purchasing department's total effort! When the team members showed this to people in purchasing, they confirmed that once a year the monitoring and expediting effort indeed rose to this high level, and hundreds of hours of overtime were devoted to it. When did this high level occur? We'll get to that later.

In their search to lower this lateness, the team realized that nearly two-thirds of all requisitions for materials and components came from the inventory control department, and one-third from the design engineering Department. They focused on those from Inventory Control. Why were these late? What could be done to get them on time?

Inventory Control Requisitions

Many years before, the company had installed a typical "order point" inventory control system, based on liberal safety stock levels acceptable at that time. As economic pressures increased, inventory levels were reduced by executive edict, and safety stock levels disappeared.

The old inventory system was not responsive enough to function without the safety stocks, so frequent stockouts occurred. When a material withdrawal order was issued for an item, the inventory stock person would look for the item, discover it was out, and send an emergency, expedited material requisition to purchasing, days late. Toward the end of each fiscal year, word went out to inventory control to reduce inventory levels in an attempt to improve the appearance of the balance sheet. Inventory analysts did not send requisitions to purchasing. No replenishing purchase orders were placed. The rate of inventory stockouts shot up. Production sagged. Expediting soared. Customers grew disgusted with continually missed shipping dates. But the year end balance sheet looked great.

Shortly after the start of the new fiscal year, hundreds of material requisitions flushed out of inventory control, all late when they arrived in purchasing. They issued the purchase orders as fast as possible, and then devoted more and more time to monitoring and expediting these orders, until this effort rose to its highest level during the first quarter of the fiscal year.

Material flowed in, inventories rose to acceptable levels, shipping performance improved. Purchase order monitoring and expediting eased off.

But then year end approached. Requisitions were held back. Few purchase orders were issued. Monitoring and expediting dropped to its lowest level at the close of the fiscal year, and they were ready to start the cycle again.

Inventory Control Improvements

The O.F.A. team concluded that major improvements were needed in the inventory control processes, and recommended the introduction of a new material requirements planning system based on forecasted order requirements instead of the old order point method. With these new systems:

- Inventory levels would be accurately monitored
- Requisitions would be sent on time from inventory control to purchasing
- Purchase orders would be sent on time from purchasing to the vendors
- The vendors would deliver the required materials on time
- Effort devoted to order monitoring and expediting would be reduced
- Overall shipping performance would be improved.

Design Engineering Requisitions

As in many equipment manufacturing businesses, design engineering prepared bills of material detailing the parts and materials needed to produce each order. When complete, these bills were released to production planning and control, which in turn issued material requisitions to purchasing for those items which they should buy for this specific order.

Every product contained certain long-lead-time components which had to be ordered before design engineering could complete and release these bills of material, and on these items design engineering issued "prerelease" requisitions directly to purchasing. Essentially all requisitions issued by design engineering were of this type.

Why were these prerelease requisitions late? Was this a symptom of problems in engineering? If so, what were they?

Members of the O.F.A. team reviewed their interview notes, and discussed this with the people from engineering who issued the prerelease requisitions. They received this answer:

Sure, we know we're late in issuing many of the prerelease requisitions. We don't like it any better than you do, but we can't really do a thing about it. All of our design work depends on the customer specs we get from the inside sales department, and they're nearly always late in sending that information to us. There's not much we can do to issue those prerelease requisitions to purchasing earlier, unless we can get the customer specs earlier from inside sales. They sit on those specs until every last detail is in before they send them to us. There's your problem. Better go see them.

So the team members did just that. After they described the situation to the manager of inside sales, they got an answer from him. What was it? You guessed it:

Well, we'd love to send those customer specs to engineering sooner. In fact, in the past year we've introduced several new methods that have knocked out about a week from our processing time here in inside sales. But that didn't help much, because the real problem is that we don't get those customer orders and specs soon enough from field sales.

I've never really understood why they take so long to firm up an order, but they do. Information on a particular order strings in from field sales over a period of two or three months. Often several changes are made from the time we get a piece of information until we finally release the complete spec to engineering. We're never sure when we are going to get what. Sometimes the information we need first comes last, and vice versa.

So we just wait until we get everything from field sales before we release any of it to engineering. That's the only safe way. The real problem is out there in field sales. Talk with them and see if you can straighten them out.

The team was lucky. During the next couple of weeks, three field salesmen visited the plant, and the team members cornered each one and discussed this situation with him. They all expressed their concern. In the words of one of them:

This is an old problem. We've tried to solve it for years, but we've concluded nothing can be done about it. Our equipment is integrated with larger pieces of equipment which the customer's engineers specify first, before they specify ours. They've always done it that way. We surely wouldn't want to ask the customers to change their design process just for the convenience of some of our design engineers here at the plant.

The O.F.A. team was not put off. They realized that just because it had always been that way in the past, did not mean it had to be that way in the future. Considering this further, they concluded that the basic problem was that the sequence of *receipt* of customer information was inconsistent with the sequence of *use* of this information in the engineering, purchasing, and manufacturing processes. To make matters worse, this inconsistency was not understood by the people who could influence it most, that is, the field salesmen and the customers.

Team members, working with people from purchasing and design engineering, developed a master schedule for the flow of customer specifications into the business so that the sequence of the receipt of information would be consistent with the sequence of use. They discussed this schedule with the field salesmen and customers, and demonstrated how such a consistent flow would improve the company's shipping performance, and significantly benefit all customers. Once the customers and field salesmen understood these potential benefits, they contributed their ideas to this approach, and a balanced answer was developed.

SUMMARY

As illustrated in Figure 17.3, a detailed analysis of purchasing department activities led to the realization that missed shipments on the manufacturing factory floor were largely caused by late material purchases. However, this was not caused by problems in the purchasing department. Rather, it was the result of two basic factors.

First, the inventory control system for stock materials and components was obsolete, and was misused at year end.

Second, the sequence of flow of information from field sales was inconsistent with the use of that information in engineering, purchasing, and manufacturing.

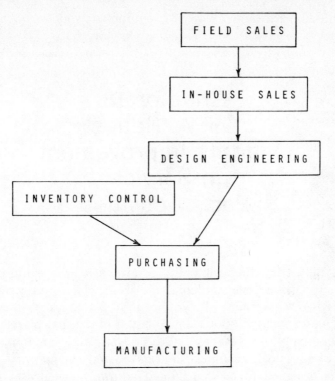

Figure 17.3

When the problems in inventory control and field sales were solved, the problem of missed shipments on the manufacturing factory floor was solved.

This case demonstrates the importance of demand identification and modification, and interdepartmental analysis of work flow in knowledge work productivity improvement.

Chapter 18
O.F.A. Ratios
Quantify Improvement
in Service
Parts Activities

In many industries, the availability of after-sale service and parts is a major factor in selecting the company from which you want to buy your original equipment. If you cannot get parts to service the product, you surely will not want to buy it in the first place.

The company in this case study was in such an industry. Its products had a high technical content, lasted for many years, and had parts designed to be "consumed" during normal use. For this reason, its customers commonly ordered parts for equipment many years old, and expected the company to provide them promptly.

MANAGEMENT OBJECTIVES

Before ordering parts, most customers sent inquiries requesting a quotation on price and delivery. Customers were increasingly dissatisfied because they felt it took too long to get the requested quotations. They were especially disturbed because their equipment was often inoperative while waiting for these quotations and the subsequent delivery of parts. This had grown worse until some long-time customers had threatened to buy their parts *and* original equipment from other vendors unless these quotations could be provided more rapidly.

Therefore, as part of a larger O.F.A. program, senior managers wanted their O.F.A. team to review the handling of parts inquiries, identify problems, and recommend solutions.

INITIAL REVIEW

As the first step, O.F.A. team members conducted a scoping interview with the manager of the parts department. When they asked him about the need for faster response to inquiries, he said that their response time was good. On the average, for all inquiries, it was less than four hours. Half of the inquiries were answered immediately while the customer was still on the telephone. The other inquiries were more complex, but even those were answered in a little over four days on the average.

. The team members agreed that sounded reasonable. However when they discussed this with the manager of marketing they got a different story. He agreed the average response time was OK; that was not the problem. Customers were pleased to receive a quote immediately, or within a few days in some cases. However, they could not understand why other inquiries might take weeks, even months, for no apparent reason. Some inquiries just seemed to get lost in the organization, while their equipment remained out of operation; this made the customers mad.

INQUIRY WORK FLOW

Team members continued their interviews and prepared the functional flow diagram in Figure 18.1. The company received three types of inquiries. As shown on the far left, parts analysts received about 200 telephone inquiries each month ($V = 200$) for which they could determine price and delivery from their own records, while the customer remained on the telephone. This function, quotation preparation — pricing, consumed about 22 hours per month ($H = 22$), or 0.1 hours per each inquiry ($R = 0.1$).

They received another 50 telephone inquiries each month which required more effort. These were documented and combined with 150 other inquiries received by mail, and were logged through the function, inquiry control.

The parts analysts then reviewed each inquiry to determine the technical basis for the quotation, that is, what specific parts were needed, drawing numbers, etc. In 140 cases out of the 200, they were able to complete this technical review on their own, after which they priced and documented the quotation, and sent it to the customer.

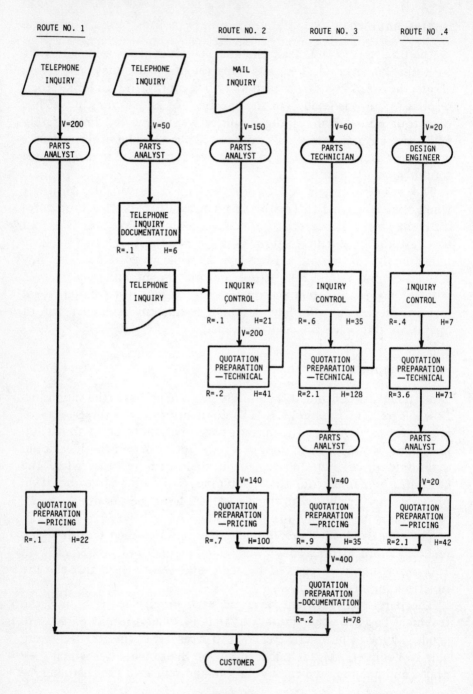

Figure 18.1

The parts analysts could not determine the technical basis for quoting on the remaining 60, and, therefore, sent these to more skilled specialists — the parts technicians.

The parts technicians logged these in, and conducted their technical review. In 40 out of the 60, they were able to determine the required technical information, after which they returned the inquiry to the parts analysts, who priced, documented and sent the quotation to the customer.

As shown on the far right of Figure 18.1, for the final 20 inquiries, the parts technicians were unable to determine the necessary technical information, so they sent these inquiries to the design engineering group. After an engineer had defined the technical data for the requested parts, the inquiry was returned to the parts analysts, who completed the process as shown.

Differences in Effort

The team then reviewed this diagram, totaled the O.F.A. ratios, and determined the effort in man-hours needed to process each type of inquiry, shown in Table 18.1 Although they had anticipated the short time required for the telephone inquiries that could be handled immediately through route 1, they were very surprised by the differences between routes 2, 3, and 4.

When they summarized the data, and calculated the total effort devoted to each route (Table 18.2), they realized that although the 60 inquiries going through routes 3 and 4 were only 15% of the total volume, they accounted for 65% of the total processing effort in man-hours!

Differences in Elapsed Cycle Time

The team members then examined the log sheets prepared by the parts analysts which showed the elapsed cycle time for each inquiry, that is, how long it was in house from the time the inquiry was received until the quotation was sent out.

Data from their sample is in Table 18.3. By multiplying the volume of inquiries per month by the average elapsed cycle time per inquiry, they determine a cumulative elapsed time for each route. In this way, they had a general measure of the impact the inquiries in each route had on the problem of inquiry response time.

Table 18.1. O.F.A. Ratios for Inquiry Processing.

TYPE OF INQUIRY	HOURS CONSUMED PER INQUIRY
1. Telephone inquiry handled immediately by parts analyst	0.1 = 0.1
2. Mail inquiry handled by parts analyst	0.1 + 0.2 + 0.7 + 0.2 = 1.2
3. Mail inquiry handled by parts analyst and technician	0.1 + 0.2 + 0.6 + 2.1 + 0.9 + 0.2 = 4.1
4. Mail inquiry handled by parts analyst, technician, and design engineer	0.1 + 0.2 + 0.6 + 2.1 + 0.4 + 3.6 + 2.1 + 0.2 = 9.3

NOTE: Telephone inquiries that pass through routes 2, 3, and 4 require 0.1 hours more than the effort shown here for the mail inquiries.

Table 18.2. Inquiry Processing Effort, Current Conditions.

ROUTE NUMBER	INQUIRIES PER MONTH	HOURS PER INQUIRY	HOURS PER MONTH
1	200	0.1	20
2	140	1.2	168
3	40	4.1	164
4	20	9.3	186
			538

Table 18.3. Inquiry Processing Elapsed Time, Current Conditions.

ROUTE NUMBER	INQUIRIES PER MONTH	ELAPSED TIME PER INQUIRY	CUMULATIVE ELAPSED TIME IN DAYS
1	200	6 min.	0.83
2	140	1.9 days	266.
3	40	5.2 days	208.
4	20	21.1 days	422.
			897.

As before, the team members were struck by routes 3 and 4, where the 60 inquiries made up 15% of the volume, but 70% of the cumulative elapsed cycle time! Furthermore, they realized that the increase in elapsed cycle time between routes 1 and 4 was much greater than the increase in processing effort. Although the processing effort increased only 8.1 man-hours (Table 18.2), the elapsed cycle time increased 19 days (Table 18.3), nearly one calendar month!

EVALUATION

The team members by now realized that the large effort and cycle time consumed by some inquiries was due to the great amount of technical review in routes 3 and 4. This led them to ask:

- Why are 30% of the 200 inquiries that start through route 2 eventually transferred to routes 3 and 4 for additional technical review? (What is the nature of the demand?)
- What information or knowledge do the parts technicians and design engineers have that the parts analysts do not?
- What can be done to reduce the need for this technical review, and to simplify the quotation process?

At first, the team assumed that the inquiries which needed a lot of technical review were for obsolete parts. However, a sample showed that the majority of inquiries in routes 3 and 4 were for parts still in current production, many of them in the parts inventory, ready for immediate shipment!

After further analysis, the team concluded there were two major reasons that inquiries passed through routes 3 and 4, both the result of old habits.

First, customers did not order parts properly. Service manuals with detailed descriptions of parts were supplied with all products, and could be replaced if lost. Using these manuals, customers requesting quotations could easily identify the parts by number.

Many customers did not want to bother with this, so they simply asked for a quotation on "the big red lever on the back of the control panel on our machine we bought from you in 1957." Most of the technical review consisted of examining old order records, identifying the equipment serial number, locating parts manuals, bills of material, and drawings, and finally identifying the part number. What took a parts technician or even a design engineer hours to do, could have been done by the customer in a few minutes.

The second reason that many inquiries passed through routes 3 and 4 was the unavailability of records, coupled with narrow, parochial attitudes. For years, parts technicians had accumulated a body of informal records based on their more technical background. This gave them a technical superiority over the parts analysts. In short, these were "technician's records," by and for them alone. Similarly, some of the design engineers had their personal, informal records, which by tradition were used only by the design engineers.

These long-standing practices and attitudes forced inquiries into routes 3 and 4 much more often than really was necessary. To make matters worse, the parts technicians and design engineers had many other responsibilities, so they viewed these inquiries as secondary demands, to be worked on when convenient. Hence the increase in elapsed processing time was much greater than the increase in actual applied working time.

IMPROVEMENT

The O.F.A. team recommended a two-part improvement. First, field salesmen, along with parts department people, began an intensive campaign to ensure that customers retained and learned to use their service parts manuals as ordering guides. The pricing structure was changed to favor those who did this.

Second, a program was started to document and disperse the internal parts records. That is, the informal records heretofore kept by the parts technicians and engineers were documented and made available to everyone. This enabled the parts analysts to answer many inquiries previously routed through the technicians and engineers.

On this basis, the team members and parts manager estimated that 70% of the inquiries passing through design engineering could be handled by the parts analysts, while at least 60% of those handled by the technicians could in the future be handled by the analysts. As shown in Tables 18.4 and 18.5, this would result in a 26% reduction in processing effort, and a 34% reduction in cumulative elapsed processing cycle time. Thus, these improvements would lead to better internal productivity, customer satisfaction, and future sales of both parts and new equipment.

Table 18.4. Inquiry Processing Effort, Improved Conditions.

ROUTE NUMBER	INQUIRIES PER MONTH	HOURS PER INQUIRY	HOURS PER MONTH
1	200	0.1	20
2	164	1.2	197
3	30	4.1	123
4	6	9.3	56
			396

Improvement = $\dfrac{538 - 396}{538}$ = 26%

Table 18.5. Inquiry Processing Elapsed Time, Improved Conditions.

ROUTE NUMBER	INQUIRIES PER MONTH	ELAPSED TIME PER INQUIRY	CUMULATIVE ELAPSED TIME IN DAYS
1	200	6 min.	0.83
2	164	1.9 days	311.6
3	30	5.2 days	156.0
4	6	21.1 days	126.6
			595.

Improvement = $\dfrac{897 - 595}{897}$ = 34%

SUMMARY

This case demonstrated again the value of viewing work flow in terms of alternate routes, and then calculating the O.F.A. ratios to measure the relative effort for each route. Once this was done, the O.F.A. team modified both the demands and the functions to reduce the effort.

This case also presented an evaluation of processing cycle time, which in many businesses is at least as important as processing effort.

Index